CUSTER

CUSTER'S BUGLER
The Life of John Martin
(Giovanni Martino)

Leo Solimine

Universal-Publishers
Boca Raton

Custer's Bugler: The Life of John Martin (Giovanni Martino)

Copyright © 2012 Leo Solimine
All rights reserved.

Universal-Publishers
Boca Raton, Florida • USA
2012

ISBN-10: 1-61233-084-3
ISBN-13: 978-1-61233-084-6

www.universal-publishers.com

Cover photo "Civil War Bugler"
© Ed Brennan | Dreamstime.com
Cover photo "Little Bighorn Battlefield"
© David Lloyd | Dreamstime.com

Library of Congress Cataloging-in-Publication Data

Solimine, Leo, 1960-
Custer's bugler : the life of John Martin (Giovanni Martino) / Leo
Solimine.
    pages cm
Includes bibliographical references.
ISBN 978-1-61233-084-6 (pbk. : alk. paper) -- ISBN 1-61233-084-3
(pbk. : alk. paper)
    1. Martin, John, 1851 or 1852-1922. 2. Little Bighorn, Battle of the,
Mont., 1876. 3. United States. Army. Cavalry, 7th--Biography. 4. Soldiers--United States--Biography. 5. Italian American soldiers--
Biography. 6. Buglers--United States--Biography. I. Title.
E83.876.S76 2012
973.8'2092--dc23
[B]
                                                              2011050057

CONTENTS

Trumpeter John Martin (born Giovanni Crisostimo Martino) in a photograph taken by David F. Barry in 1904. Martin's uniform bears six service stripes corresponding with his thirty years of continuous service and three medals. Seventh Cavalry records enlistment records indicate he had hazel eyes, dark hair and stood 5' 6".

Introduction

Custer leaned forward in his saddle and intently studied the Indian village stretched across the valley below. His battalion of five companies from the U.S. Seventh Cavalry Regiment had just halted on a high ridge overlooking the Little Bighorn River. As officers peered through field glasses, a few of them remarked on the size of the village; across the river, as far as they could see, hundreds upon hundreds of tepees carpeted the valley floor. After weeks of hard riding, General George Custer and the Seventh Cavalry had found their quarry.

"These hills and bluffs hid most of the village from us," observed the General as he scanned the valley through his field glasses. Lieutenant William Cooke, Custer's experienced adjutant, nodded as his eyes shifted from the massive village to his commander.

"We got them this time," Custer exclaimed to Cooke and the officers. "We got 'em!" He turned in the saddle and waved his hat to the waiting troopers. "Hurrah, boys, we've got them!" he shouted. "We'll finish them up and then go home to our station!" Over two hundred troopers and scouts replied with three dust-choked cheers.

Custer rejoined the battalion and led them at a gallop for a mile along the bluffs. As they reached a wide ravine that emptied into the river and valley below, Custer once gain halted the battalion. Instinctively, Cooke nudged his mount closer to Custer while the troopers dismounted and adjusted their saddles; a few checked their weapons in preparation for the fight ahead. Overhead, the Montana sun blazed across a cloudless sky, a slight breeze offered little relief to the sweating troopers and horses.

"We need Benteen and the packs now," Custer snapped. "Send another messenger!" Cooke motioned and a young trooper quickly responded, a brass bugle across his back dangled as he trotted up to the General.

Custer spoke rapidly, "Orderly, I want you to take a message to Benteen. Ride as fast as you can and tell him to hurry. Tell him it's a big village and I want him to be quick, and to bring the ammunition packs." The orderly saluted and turned his mount back up the trail.

"Wait, orderly," Cooke shouted, "I'll give you a message." Sweat streamed from the Lieutenant's thick beard as he hurriedly wrote into a field pad. He ripped out the page and handed it to the orderly. "Ride as fast as you can to Benteen. Take the same trail we came down," he instructed, "If you have time and there is no danger, come back; but otherwise stay with your company."

The orderly took the dispatch and nodded, then spurred his horse back up the trail. A few moments later, he crested a ridge and looked back. He watched the long column of Seventh Cavalry troopers follow Custer into the ravine, Cooke trailed behind at a brisk trot, until they disappeared, swallowed by a cloud of dust. As Custer and his men rode to their fate, the orderly - John Martin – turned back to the trail, focused on finding Benteen and delivering Custer's final desperate message.

On June 25-26, 1876, the largest engagement of the short-lived Great Sioux War - the Battle of the Little Bighorn - was fought by a stream in the southeastern corner of the Montana Territory. The United States Seventh Cavalry Regiment, led by Lieutenant Colonel George Armstrong Custer, expected to crush a determined and well-armed force of 4,000 Sioux warriors. The unexpected outcome shocked the nation: Custer, Cooke and 210 cavalrymen were overwhelmed and quickly annihilated by the banks of the Little Bighorn River while two other Seventh Regiment battalions endured a two-day ordeal on a barren hilltop three miles away. When it finally ended, more than 268 troopers and scouts had perished. John Martin was not among them: his life saved by a piece of paper, Custer's final desperate message.

The Battle of the Little Bighorn propelled John Martin into the national spotlight. Before the battle, John Martin was an anonymous Seventh Regiment trooper, a bugler for Company H. A fateful reassignment on the morning of June 25 placed him at the center of "the most written-about battle in our history, after all — more than Gettysburg, which was far more important in the grand scheme of things."[1] The battle remains etched in our collective history, examined as much for its myths as for the many controversies surrounding it. The comprehensive research extends beyond strategic and tactical concerns to include intensive analyses of the men who played a major role: George Armstrong Custer, Frederick Benteen, Marcus Reno, Sitting Bull, and Crazy Horse. Much less is known about the last messenger, a young Italian immigrant named John Martin, who "... played a conspicuous part in the celebrated battle."[2]

Journalists of the period popularized the myth of Giovanni Martini (Martin's assumed original name): the former drummer boy for Garibaldi and, later, heroic bugler for the Seventh Cavalry. They faithfully, if not necessarily accurately, labeled him as 'Sole Survivor of Custer's Massacre' and the 'last white man to see Custer alive.'[3] In reality, he may have been neither. Even his assumed original surname of Martini is inaccurate, and disproven by the discovery of documentary evidence.

After the Little Bighorn, everyone *knew* John Martin's story. Or, thought they did. Tracing John Martin's life proved a complex task, primarily due to the sporadic documentation available coupled with his particular circumstances. A myriad of sources were utilized to recreate most of his life: Interviews, newspaper articles, civil records, enlistment papers, family recollections, transcripts from a military inquiry, and even a mysterious diary. Any narration or chronicle of John Martin's life demands a measure of reconstruction and the void periods, especially his early years, necessitated the prudent use of conjecture and speculation, properly tamed by the historical record. When combined with the existing documentation, a credible and sustainable tale began to emerge. The true story of his life was more fascinating and enigmatic than any myth set forth by journalists.

PART I

THE EARLY YEARS

CHAPTER ONE

A Foundling in Sala

On the morning of January 28, 1852, Maria d'Amelio heard a familiar sound from the back of her home and hurried to the source. In a niche against the wall that once held a window, a horizontal wooden wheel creaked as it slowly turned; attached to its top was a small round cabinet that covered a cradle. When the wheel stopped rotating, a small bell rang out and a baby nestled in the cradle whimpered softly in reply.

Another infant had been abandoned: Left on the "wheel" (*la ruota*) by the mother. Maria scooped up and examined the baby, a boy, and she estimated he was perhaps a month old. The baby was dressed in rags with only a dirty white bonnet protecting his head from the cold. Sometimes the mothers left a note or small religious medal with the infant, but Maria found nothing in the cradle.

The infant's arrival set in motion a familiar and efficient routine in Sala. Within the next few hours, the baby boy acquired a new name and received the Catholic Sacrament of Holy Baptism. At 4:00 p.m., the final step was completed in the Town Hall. With the Mayor, Maria and several witnesses in attendance, a clerk recorded the boy's name in a Civil Register: The *Comune* (town) of Sala officially welcomed their newest citizen, Giovan Crisostimo Martino.[1] By that evening, little Giovan was asleep in the home of a wet nurse.

Many infants had preceded him through *la ruota* at Maria's home, and more would follow; her residence served as the *Proietti domiciliata* (Home for Foundlings or Abandoned Children) for the Comune of Sala. As an idiom, the Italian word, *proietto* ('projectile'), implies an expulsion, or (something) to be cast out; the word also applied to foundlings and abandoned infants. The tragedy of abandonment occurred with enough frequency that most Italian cities and towns, including Sala, established homes to provide a safe haven for the helpless infants.[2]

The problem of widespread abandonment was neither restricted to the Italian peninsula nor the nineteenth century: "Infant abandonment was a prominent feature of life in much of Europe since Roman times."[3] In ancient Rome, unwanted infants faced a precarious future, and many were left to perish in the forest. Others were abandoned by a column in a forum in they would be found and raised by another Roman citizen; yet even these infants, if they survived, usually faced a life of slavery and servitude. The blight of abandonment continued into the Middle Ages. Troubled by the "great numbers of bodies of newborns ... regularly appearing in the nets of the fishermen trolling" the Tiber River, Pope Innocent III - who reigned from 1198 until 1216 - established the first foundling homes in Rome. He hoped to ensure "... they were baptized before they died."[4]

No single explanation sufficed for the practice of institutionalized abandonment.[5] Factors ranged from family and societal pressure to overwhelming financial hardship. The rural agrarian society of nineteenth-century Italy centered on the family unit. A patriarchal system, the father guided the family's living and guarded its interests aggressively in a dangerous world. The family's traditions and income were subject to his control, and family members could expect to have their roles rigidly defined. The façade of family honor had to be maintained; any threat to it – and, by extension, the father's authority – was expelled. In most Italian communities, and especially true in Sala, families lived in close proximity to each other. Secrecy served as a protective barrier and great efforts were made to keep the shame of premarital and out-of-wedlock pregnancies hidden.

Safe and effective birth control did not exist in this period. Once born, the illegitimate infants were often unwanted or rejected by the family. Faced with the loss of their only support system, mothers had little choice but to abandon their newborns and many were "left on the doorstep of a church to be raised by the church or put in an orphanage."[6] If shunned by their families, expectant mothers traveled to neighboring villages or cities to deliver their babies - with the help of a midwife - before leaving the newborns at the local foundling home.[7] Married women often faced a similar dilemma as the resources of their impoverished families were stretched too far by the birth of another child, and were not immune to using *la ruota*. For an established fee, local midwives provided temporary accommodations and assisted with the birth; as the mother returned to her home, the newborn was deposited at a local foundling home. The issue of abandonment created a ruthless paradox, one that found a family-centered society so willing to cast off its unwanted members.

In Sala and other southern Italian towns, most of the population consisted of poor peasants who toiled as sharecroppers (*contadini*) and day laborers (*giornalieri*); a smaller subset included low-level artisans and shopkeepers. A subsistence barter system formed the basis of the local economy and hard currency was not a prevalent aspect of most transactions. The city-state system was in its final days, yet to be supplanted by a unified Italian republic. In theory, the feudal period had ended, but in villages like Sala, the true authority and power remained "... concentrated in the hands of a few owners with landless peasants working the soil."[8] Unlike regions in the north of Italy, landowners in the south possessed enormous tracts of land. While a few landowners, mostly rich families, lived locally on their vast estates, many remained far away from the Vallo (valley) di Diano, and guided their business affairs as absentee landlords. Wealthy families vied with the Church as the largest landowners in southern Italy. The arrangement was the source of great resentment by the *contadini* towards the Church, who received little compassion or charity from their local parishes.

A few families were able to acquire small parcels of farmland, yet most were relegated to work as sharecroppers for prosperous landowners. The farms (*podere*) often consisted of several hundred acres, and required several families and day laborers to work their fields. Landowners compensated families with homes and a portion of the farm's annual profits. An observer in southern Italy during the mid-nineteenth century noted the annual yield in most *podere* was often valued at less than $200, half of which was shared with *contadino*. The arrangement was less appealing, the observer continued, because the *contadino's* families - "eight or nine children being by no means an uncommon number" - ensured the share was never sufficient.[9] Single men without homes or families, often former foundlings, roamed the farms seeking work as day laborers in exchange for money, food or a place to live.

Households reliant on agriculture for their primary subsistence braved the perpetual uncertainty of the harvest. With many mouths and unable to preserve their food stores, any crop failure could prove disastrous. A successful harvest allowed households to trade for desperately needed provisions, while a poor one drained their meager resources. Charities were limited in availability and resources. There was little margin between survival and starvation. When the arrival of an infant distressed the household economy, the father's options were few and the threat to the family's well-being was resolved by a visit to *la ruota*. In their desperate circumstances, sacrifice for the family's preservation could apply to their own (legitimate) children. Church-sponsored homes for abandoned children had existed for over six hundred years in many cities throughout the Italy. Often poorly funded, the large institutional orphanages housed hundreds in harsh and unsanitary conditions. Orphans fared no better than foundlings, and little distinction made in their treatment and expectations. Smaller towns eventually established alternate shelters to handle the influx of abandoned children, and in towns like Sala, homes like Maria d'Amelio's *Proietti domiciliata* for foundlings (*trovatelli*) began to appear. Not all functioned as permanent residences; cost constraints forced many to serve as temporary accommodations until a more permanent home was found, as in the case of little Giovan. The rapidity of his placement – within the same day as his 'discovery' - indicated Maria's home operated as a way station or drop off point.

To protect the mother's identity and provide a safe refuge for the infant, foundling homes – modeling cloistered convents - installed a simple rotating wooden mechanism: *la ruota* (wheel). A wooden wheel laid on its side replaced a low window; affixed to the wheel was a small cradle or cabinet. A long wooden pin held the wheel in place as it revolved. As the newborn was placed in the open cradle, the mother or midwife rotated the wheel, and the baby revolved into the home; to notify the attendant of the new arrival, a small bell hanging by the wheel was rung.[10]

After the infant was left at the foundling home, a well-established process of municipal registration commenced. Civic officials tasked with naming the foundlings acted quickly since the baptism that immediately followed – in the Catholic tradition – required the baby to have a name. Foundling surnames ranged from the creative and well meaning (*Innocenti* or Innocent) to generic and bland, even derogatory: *Trovato* (Found), *Sventura* (Unfortunate), and, *Brutto* (Ugly). Esposito, the most common surname in Naples, derived from "the practice among the orphanages of displaying the orphans to visitors." Often, the public viewing facilitated - not a benevolent adoption - but an opportunity for wealthy families to choose which of the "… orphans could be taken into the homes as servants."[11] An awful pattern emerged for foundlings: If they survived infancy, a life of servitude likely awaited.

With an urgent need to nourish the newborns, municipal officials turned to a network of local wet nurses. Women who had recently given birth, and therefore able to breastfeed, were contacted. Infant mortality rates in the region neared the 50th percentile; a circumstance that proved beneficial as it increased the pool of available wet nurses to include mothers who lost infants to an early death. The wet nurses were paid for their services by the Comune.[12] Compensatory payments, often less than 25 lire a month by one estimate, varied by city and town with northern Italian areas paying more than their poorer southern counterparts.[13] As they grew, the foundlings usually continued to live with the wet nurse; however, rarely did the family of the wet nurse legally adopt the infant. With another mouth to feed, households that assumed guardianship expected more than the Comune's inadequate compensation; when the children reached maturity, they were put to work in the fields.[14] Not all of the abandoned children remained in Sala, however, and those not 'adopted' into a family were transported directly to institutional orphanages in Naples.[15]

Perhaps by design, the *Comuni* (pluralized form of *comune*) assumed a minor role as labor provider for their regions. Political upheaval and poor harvests created a difficult situation for most peasants. Troubled by the turmoil and potential threat to their income, landowners increased rents and reduced payments; many sharecroppers were forced off their land to an even worse fate as part of the ever-growing legion of "landless day laborers" seeking employment.[16] Although a ready supply of laborers was available, most households lacked the financial means to pay for their services. A solution lay, often quite literally, at their doorstep in the form of foundlings. While not explicitly endorsing the use of foundlings as chattel and slave labor, civil administrators shared the community's need to remain viable. The land demanded their hard labor, and after reaching maturation, foundlings provided a small, steady and inexpensive source of workers. As more foundlings were placed into 'foster' homes, the reduced cost - fewer homes to maintain and decreased compensation for wet nurses and "adopting" families – benefitted the Comune, but not the unfortunate *trovatelli*.

CHAPTER TWO

Searching the Civil Records

Persistent tales in Sala of John Martin and the Little Bighorn intrigued Professor Giuseppe Colitti, an expert in Italian oral history and traditions.[1] He surmised that the abundance of local lore must have been based on some bit of fact, and wondered if proof confirming Sala Consilina as Martin's birthplace existed. Other regions in Italy claimed Martin as one of their own; the most persistent came from Apricale, a small village in the far western region of Liguria. Most evidence, however, indicated Sala as his birthplace, yet the primary source for this information - John Martin - vacillated on the subject in later interviews. As an abandoned infant, Martin truly did not know where he was born. His mother may have traveled from a neighboring town to hide her pregnancy; without definitive knowledge, Martin may not have considered the question of his birthplace important. The same reasoning can be applied to queries of his actual date of birth. Ultimately, Colitti needed confirmation to substantiate the Sala claim and his search began in Sala's town hall, the central repository of the Comune's vital records.

Primary sources for births in Italy during the nineteenth century are limited to civil and parish records, especially in provincial towns like Sala. An unlikely benefactor, Napoleon Bonaparte, ushered in modern standards for Italian civil records. During the French Empire's administration of the Italian peninsula, the Bonaparte system of civil control and records was implemented.[2] Long after Napoleon's exile, his system of civil recordation remained. In Sala, a civil official (*ufficiale dello stato civile*) documented all major life events – births, marriages and deaths – as required by civil code. The records, often duplicated, remain an excellent source of information, unlike parish records, especially in southern Italy. Parish birth records lacked the informative quality of civil documents and until the early 1900s, only originals were recorded; many have been lost, stolen or damaged by flood or fire, rendering them unreadable at best.[3]

Due to their age, Sala's civil records are carefully maintained and rarely exhibited, a consequence of the effort to preserve them. Paper documents have deteriorated and ink has "[f]aded or been rendered illegible by humidity and time."[4] In time, digitization will allow greater access, but for the present, tremendous care is taken to ensure preservation of these important records, including enactment of laws restricting public viewing. Pursuant to the Comune's policies for accessing the archives, a civil official from Sala, Dr. Michele Esposito, was assigned to assist Professor Colitti.[5] Steeped in the history and culture of Sala Consilina, Esposito's experience with the *Comune's* civil records would prove useful. In 1997, Colitti and Esposito began an extensive investigation for any information relating to Martin's birth.[6]

Beginning with the most commonly accepted (original) surname of Martini, their initial examination of civil birth records in Sala failed to produce any males born between 1851 and 1853; an earlier search of records in Rome with similar parameters was equally futile.[7] In a typical birth registration at Sala's town hall, a civil official certified that both parents were present and the infant's birth was recorded in the Civil Register for Acts of Birth (*Registri dello Stato Civile, Atti di Nascita*). Recordation of foundlings, however, required an alternate set of protocols, including a different birth register. Esposito's familiarity with Sala's archives aided in their hunt and a set of records dedicated to foundling births was found. As they pored through the 50 kilogram leather-bound register, their preliminary search for a foundling named Martini was unsuccessful, but a subsequent review produced an interesting discovery: Entitled *Atto di Nascita di Esposizione di un Bambino Proietto* (Act of Birth for an Abandoned Child), the document registered the birth of Giovan Crisostimo Martino.

Colitti and Esposito were confident that the Martino record found in Sala's archives belonged to John Martin, but one difference loomed. A common misperception maintains that Martini was John Martin's original surname. The Sala birth register for Giovan Martino apparently disproved this notion and to validate their discovery, Colitti and Esposito needed independent confirmation. Help arrived in the form of Claudio Busi, a freelance researcher and author from Italy.[8] His interest in the Martin story began after a visit to the Little Bighorn River in 1981; he was intrigued by the tales of the Italian bugler who carried the final dispatch and survived 'Custer's Last Stand.'

Working independently, Claudio Busi focused his research on immigration records. He surmised that Martin could not have arrived in America after June 1874 (the month and year of his Army enrollment), and that Martin's port of entry was New York. Until Ellis Island opened in 1890, the immigration center at Castle Garden - also in lower Manhattan - processed new arrivals to America. Busi utilized The Battery Conservancy's Castle Garden database of immigrant registration to examine ship's manifests for male passengers with the Martini surname for the period of 1865 through 1874. The name Giovanni Martini did not appear in the immigration records, and the lone exception was a Giovanni Martini who arrived in 1870 aboard the S.S. Carrina: his age (26 years old) precluded him, however, since the John Martin who rode with Custer was verifiably younger. A subsequent review based on Giovanni's approximate age proved more successful: The ship's manifest for the S.S. Tyrian listed Giovanni Martino as a 21-year-old laborer from Italy who boarded the ship in late March 1873 in Naples. Upon landing, his name was recorded during the registration process administered by New York State officials at Castle Garden.[9]

The Tyrian manifest also confirmed the change (or Americanization) of his surname - from Martini or Martino to Martin - occurred after his arrival in 1873, but prior to his Army enlistment one year later. Immigrants to America quickly realized the societal disadvantages of being different. While language barriers hindered a seamless assimilation, foreign accents would eventually fade and immigrants expected to blend in more easily with an anglicized name. Amending his name from Giovanni Martino or Martini to John Martin is a logical modification. Later, a reversal of sorts may have occurred, and his new American surname, Martin, was "Italianized" to Martini. While never forgetting his Italian origins, he attached more significance to his current identity as John Martin, American citizen and soldier. Abandoned as a newborn, matters concerning birthplace, date of birth, and even surname carried less significance to Martin. Bolstered by Claudio Busi's discovery, Colitti and Esposito concluded that the Sala birth record for Giovan Crisostimo Martino reconciled to the known information for John Martin.

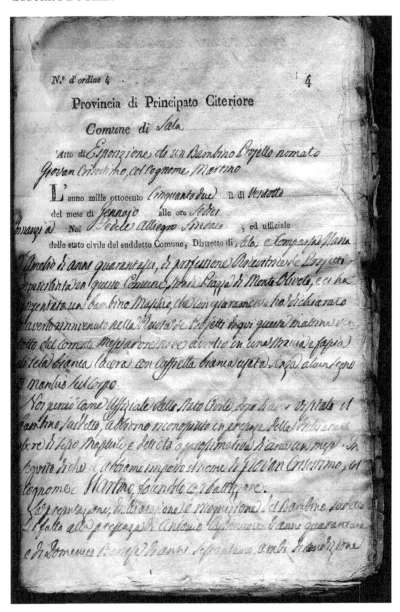

The first page of the *Atto di Nascita di Esposizione di un Bambino Proietto* (Act of Birth for an Abandoned Child) for Giovanni Crisostimo Martino from the Registry in Sala Consilina. The two-page document was located by Professor Giuseppe Colitti and Dr. Michele Esposito in 1997 in a special Register was reserved for children who had been abandoned or neglected.

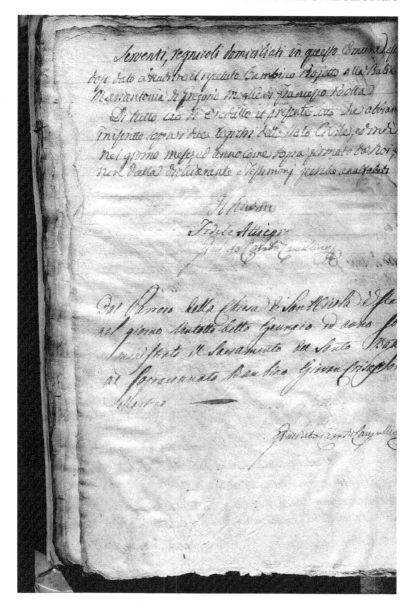

Page two of the *Atto di Nascita di Esposizione di un Bambino Proietto* (Act of Birth for an Abandoned Child) for Giovanni Crisostimo Martino. These reproductions were provided through the courtesy of Giuseppe Colitti and Michele Esposito.

The two pages of the *Atto di Nascita di Esposizione di un Bambino Proietto* (Act of Birth for an Abandoned Child) revealed details of Martin's early life. Despite slight water damage and deterioration, the document is legible and remains in moderately good condition. While portions are pre-printed, most of the form was written long-hand in Italian. Dated January 28, 1852, the opening paragraph of the *Atto di Nascita* register declared that Mayor (*Sindaco*) Fedele Alliegro and Maria d'Amelio presented to the Civil Clerk a male infant. Maria's profession - 'Receiver' at the Comune of Sala's home for abandoned children (*Proietti domiciliata*) - and age are noted. The *Proietti domiciliata's* address was included, perhaps an indication that several homes in Sala that functioned as homes like Maria's. While Maria's age (46 years old) precluded her as a wet nurse, she may have served as a local midwife,[10] and possibly helped to deliver Giovan. The urgency to record Giovan's vital data was driven by civil legislation that required all babies, regardless of circumstance, to be registered within a day of their birth (or, in this case, his "discovery"). The first paragraph concluded with a description of the child's clothing: Giovan was dressed in rags, his head topped by a filthy white bonnet. The birth document noted that the baby was *senza alcun segno e marchio sul corpo* (without any identifying mark or birthmark). Occasionally, a small token was left with the child – a form of identification, perhaps a note or religious medal - in the event that the mother regretted her decision and tried to reclaim the child, or if the family's financial situation improved. The second paragraph confirmed the baby's gender and approximate age of one month, but weight and height are unrecorded. The Clerk added that two Sala residents witnessed the registration, as required by civil code, and the *Atto di Nascita* recorded their names and ages.[11]

Obliged in his civic duty to name the child - and with a spiritual imperative to baptize him without delay – Alliegro apparently based the boy's name on two Saints of the Catholic Church. On the previous day, the Churches of Sala celebrated the Feast (or Holy Day) of Saint Giovanni Crisostimo and, thus, the boy had a first name. Colitti found determining Alliegro's choice for surname's origin a more complex matter. Drawing on his extensive experience in oral traditions, he observed rural Italians often referred to the entire month of November as *Sandu Martinu*. The name *Sandu Martinu* derives from Santo Martino (or Saint Martin) whose Feast (or Holy Day) is celebrated on November 11. The *Sandu Martinu* form of 'Santo Martino' accurately reflects the dialect spoken in the Campania region. Colitti speculated that Alliegro believed little Giovan was older than one month, and chose the surname Martino in deference to Saint Martin. Perhaps his choice of Martino suggested that the Mayor possessed specific knowledge of Giovan's circumstances, and knew the baby was born in November. One consideration for Alliegro's selection may involve a southern Italian tradition; specifically, a superstitious ritual in which Saint Martin's name (*Sandu Martinu*) is invoked before entering and leaving a bakery. If Alliegro chose the surname Martino on this basis, it was a benevolent act since the name did not draw attention to little Giovan's abandonment. Based on the evidence, Professor Colitti concluded that John Martin was born in or near Sala Consilina between November 1851 and early January 1852. While Alliegro's choice of Martino suggested the birth month was November (1851), Maria d'Amelio's estimate that Giovan was approximately one month old when he was abandoned cannot be discounted, especially in light of her experience - as a Receiver at the *Proietti domiciliata* - with newborns. Conceivably, Martin's biological mother kept the baby for a short time before she left him in *la ruota*.

The register noted the infant would be housed and nourished by Mariantonia di Gregorio (Botta), wife of Francesco Botta. Her ability to breastfeed the baby implied she had recently given birth, but the fate of the infant is unknown. Although the *Atto di Nascita* neglects to mention any compensation, an arrangement to pay the Bottas for Giovan's care must have existed; stipends for the wet nurse or 'adopting' family remained in effect for a specified time, depending on the age, gender and circumstances.[12] Generally, payments for the care of girls continued longer than for boys; males were able to work at an earlier age, and therefore, be less of a financial burden to the family. The cash payments were especially valuable in the barter-driven economy of Sala.[13]

Indicative of the high illiteracy rate prevalent throughout Italy, the final line proclaimed that of those in attendance at the registration, only the Mayor was able to sign the document, and no signatures were found "... from the declarant [Maria d'Amelio] and witnesses because they are illiterate [and thus unable to sign]." A final note, appended by a local priest, confirmed the Sacrament of the Holy Baptism was administered to Giovan Crisostomo that same day at the Church of San Nicola.

Although the discovery of Martino's birth records yielded considerable information, many questions remain unanswered. While the

Little Bighorn made him a minor celebrity, interviews by journalists and researchers focused on the battle and his actions, not his origins. As an Italian peasant, Martino could expect to have only the most basic life events recorded and documented. Following his birth registration, only marriage and death awaited recordation within the Italian civil system.

His childhood years are a blank period for which Martino offered little clarification. Although his surname remained Martino, an indication that the Bottas did not legally adopt him, his status within the family remains vague.

Other than a vague diary reference, Martino provided little of his life with the Bottas. Perhaps he demurred on questions pertaining to his youth to avoid exposing the circumstances of his abandonment. His uneven replies to questions of his year and place of birth hinted to this possibility. Walter Mason Camp, an editor and researcher investigating the Battle of the Little Bighorn, reported that Martin was born in Italy - as Giovanni Martini - in January 1853.[14] In August 1922, Colonel William A. Graham, a leading Custer scholar of the period, interviewed Martin and recorded he was born in Rome in 1851.[15] While Rome was an obvious error, the birth year of 1851 was closer to the truth than 1853. Martin's great grandchildren consider January 1, 1852, as his birth date based on his own words to their parents and grandparents.[16] Since it closely matches the civil record in Sala, this may be the most accurate estimate of his true birth date.

One explanation for Martino's inexactness reflected his Italian roots: a rural culture that deemed actual dates of birth irrelevant and trivial. Martin's advanced age – nearly 70 years - during the Graham interview in 1922 may have affected his ability to recall certain details.[17] His level of comfort with each of the interviewers may have factored in to Martin's replies, but this is difficult to ascertain based solely on the transcripts. The accurate recordation of Martin's words has never been questioned, and the infallibility of the interviewers to transcribe his replies was assumed. Inadvertent minor errors during transcription of their interview notes - perhaps resulting from Martin's admittedly imperfect English - may explain some of the inconsistencies.

CHAPTER THREE

The *Contadini*

Sala Consilina is a rugged little town perched on the side of the Monti della Maddalenna in the Campania region of southwestern Italy; the town of narrow roads and endless steps overlooks the fertile fields of the Vallo di Diano. It began as the small Roman village of Consilinum. By 1850, the town was called Sala (or La Sala), but amended to its current name, Sala Consilina, during the late nineteenth century. The mountainside location reflects Roman roots when settlements were "built up high on slopes of the severe, stony mountains of the land for purposes of security against invaders, brigands, and the malaria-filled marshes of the valleys."[1]

Sala Consilina, a *Comune* (town) in the Campania region of Salerno in southern Italy. (*Courtesy of the Comune of Sala Consilina (SA)*)

The Campania region is located in the perpetually impoverished south of Italy, an area called *Il Mezzogiorno* ('midday,' a reference to the Mediterranean sun). Originating from the north, the negative connotations implied by the term, *il Mezzogiorno*, symbolize the perpetual divisions within the Italian peninsula. As the north of Italy moved towards industrialization and modernity, the south remained isolated and mostly forgotten. An inference of the south's inferiority is evident in the appellation, "the land that time forgot;" the phrase perfectly reflected northern disdain for the stagnant nature of the south's economy and culture.[2] While the Unification of Italy[3] that culminated in the 1870s inspired northern Italy, the political and social movement "had little or no effect upon the Italians living in the *Mezzogiorno.*"[4]

The problems of the south were multifaceted: "Overpopulation, lack of arable land, rising taxes, starvation all combined to produce a hopeless situation" for many Italians farmers.[5] The agrarian economic system required farmable land and demanded hard labor to cultivate it properly, but despite their best efforts, Italy was "not a particularly fertile land to work."[6] New methods and ideas pertaining to agriculture were spurned, a reflection of the dismissive and suspicious culture. "Even the plough is used very sparingly," wrote one nineteenth century observer, "the greater part of the tilling being done with that most primitive of implements, the spade."[7] The Unification threatened to change the status quo; in response, the feudal barons who owned most of the land decreased wages and payments to sharecroppers in an effort to "maintain their wealth under the new political system."[8] Working more yet earning less, sharecroppers and day laborers struggled to feed their families. Poverty dominated their lives, with little opportunity for even marginal improvement.

Complex family dynamics played a major part in their lives. The extended family formed the most important social unit. *"L'ordine della famiglia* [the family order]," observed Richard Gambino, "the unwritten but all-demanding and complex system of rules governing one's relations within, and responsibilities to, his own family ..."[9] All members worked for the good of the family's common weal; personal and individual goals were disregarded. In their patriarchal arrangement, family matters were under the purview of the father (or oldest male). As the family head, his leadership was unquestioned and he "directed with authority his sons and their families, and even his grandchildren."[10] He determined the roles of family members, including marriages, and all earnings were deposited with him. Yet, due to the extraordinary hours devoted to working the land, he was often away from the home; while he ruled the family's daily affairs with unquestioned authority, he did so often "… in a relatively passive way."[11] Upon the father's death, patriarchal authority and land conveyed to the eldest son.

Under one roof lived the entire extended family: Parents, unmarried aunts and uncles, grandparents (if living), cousins, children, and other assorted kin. In an effort to supplement their meager earnings, a few families took in boarders, mostly landless, unmarried day laborers. With annual incomes rarely exceeding $100, the *contadino* was expected to support his entire, and often large, family.[12] As the men and boys toiled in the fields, sometimes for extended periods, the *contadine* (feminine plural for *contadino*) assumed management of the household, including control of the family's finances. While women held little external power, they wielded much influence within the walls of their homes. They supported the patriarch's decisions and ensured other family members respected his authority. During the planting or harvest seasons, the women and girls joined their fathers, uncles and brothers in the fields and shared their labors for the benefit of the family. "When their day's work in the field is over, they either take out their straw platting or their knitting," commented one visitor, struck by the industrious *contadine*, "or else sit down by those old-fashioned implements, the distaff and the spindle." Every member contributed to the family's well-being, and those deemed too young to work in the fields were pressed into service "almost as soon as they can walk [to] perform small jobs about the house and yard."[13]

Many of the homes, often the property of the Church or wealthy landholders, were nearly a thousand years old and constructed from local stone and rocks. Basic in design, the interior of the homes was partitioned into several smaller rooms. The wooden front doors opened into a bake-room and its large brick oven; the bake-room functioned as a kitchen, parlor and dining area.[14] A table "of the rudest possible fashion" sat in the center of the bake-room, accompanied by a handful of straw-bottomed chairs and "perhaps a cheap print or two" on the rough walls. The small rooms that served as sleeping quarters were on the second floor. The age of the homes combined with inadequate ventilation and poorly constructed chimneys to blacken permanently the home's walls.[15] Lacking any plumbing, bodily functions were conducted outdoors or, if necessitated by extreme cold or illness, inside utilizing a chamber pot (*pitale* or *pisciaturi*). Hygienic concerns did not factor into their daily lives. Water for cooking and cleaning came from Sala's public fountains and wells, which corralled cool water from mountain springs; daily trips transported the water home by bucket or barrel.[16] Privacy was impossible, and co-existence unavoidable in their confined surroundings.

The *contadino*, noted one visitor, "is a great believer in the proverb of 'Waste not, Want not'" and never was the adage more evident than in his dress. When a coat worn by the father became "so ragged as to be literally unwearable," it was passed to the mother who would fashion a jacket for one of the sons. As the son grew and the jacket grew too small, it was passed on to a younger son. The cycle continued until the remnants, having become nothing more than rags, would find their final home as clothing for the farm's scarecrow.[17]

Despite the agrarian environment, very few lived on their farms. Most of the local population resided within the town of Sala. With the farmable tracts located down in the valley, the *contadini* descended from their homes in Sala each day to work their fields. They were often required to travel long distances to reach their lands and it was not unusual to "spend several nights a week away" from their homes.[18] Their fields yielded walnuts, figs, grapes, olives, lentils, wheat, and peaches. Not all families worked a single tract of land; some worked a series of small separated parcels stretched across the valley, thus increasing the probability of many *contadini* to work and sleep literally on their land.

Nutritionally inadequate and lacking in variety, their diets were mostly limited to coarse black bread, grains and vegetables including tomatoes, corn, lentils, beans, onions, peas and assorted wild greens. Meat was considered "too great a luxury for any day but Sunday."[19] The men consumed most of their meals in the fields, alone or with other co-workers (often, other male family members); dinner was usually the only shared family meal of the day, when possible. The peasants lacked many luxuries, yet "even the very poorest" of the *contadini*, a traveler noted, managed to "... always have a flask of wine for dinner."[20] Salt retained a significant importance in their lives, preserving food that would otherwise spoil in this era preceding refrigeration. The effects of a poor harvest might be mitigated if enough food had been stored and preserved in anticipation.

Outside of the family, the town's square (*piazza*) was the center of social and commercial activities. A church, one or two cafés, and several small shops surrounded the piazza. In the evenings, towns-people gathered near the fountain in the piazza, a common focal point for entertainers and the local band. Men sat together and dis-cussed farming as they played the traditional Italian card games of *scoppa*, *tressette*, and *bestia*. Women knitted and gossiped with neigh-bors as their children played. The entire town joined in parades and Festivals to honor an array of Catholic Saints.

Peasants received minimal education, if any. The agrarian life-style ensured their focus remained on working the land, and pushed education into a minor role. Rarely did their children attend school, and those that did left by the third grade. At eight or nine years of age, a male child was deemed mature enough to work the fields, augmenting the labor force at hand.[21] At the same age, girls began to help with daily chores around the home. The crux of educating southern Italians remained its impact on labor: Old enough to learn meant old enough to work. The astronomical illiteracy rates correlat-ed to their deep mistrust of formal education, which was viewed as a potential challenge to the father's authority. The proverb, *ben educato* (well educated), implied one was educated in the ways of the family and honor, not in the ways of the classroom and books.

While nearly all Italians were nominally members of the Holy Roman Catholic Church, their faith diverged from standard Church doctrine. Religion hardly served as a driving force or motivator, and while women might attend church services frequently, men found their way only on special occasions. Local traditions and supersti-tions - "that fault common to all ignorant people" - held greater sway over their lives than Church dogma and doctrine.[22] In Sala, with sur-vival based on a successful harvest, prayer had its limits, much like education. Prayer was commendable, but prayer alone did not guar-antee survival.[23] In the south, where the Church often served as a landlord, local priests "dispensed little charity" to the *contadini* and "expected donations or in-kind payment for every service ren-dered."[24] The irony was not lost on the *contadini*, who viewed the Church with a degree of suspicion. Ultimately, the Church - like the land - wanted more than the *contadini* could give.

CHAPTER FOUR

From Garibaldi to America

A captivating episode involving Giuseppe Garibaldi occurred when Giovan was nine years old.[1] On September 5, 1860, as his men marched north to conquer Naples during the fight for Italian unification, General Giuseppe Garibaldi made a triumphant entrance into Sala. An Italian patriot, Garibaldi returned from exile in 1848 to free the Italy from foreign control. The long battle for Italy's Unification would become immortalized as *il Risorgimento* (the Resurgence) and Garibaldi's victories made him wildly popular among Italians, especially the peasants.

Assembling a small force of 1,000 men – the *Spedizione dei Mille* (Expedition of the 1,000) – Garibaldi invaded and conquered Sicily in May 1860. After crossing the Straits of Messina, his small army marched north to Naples, intending to overthrow the Bourbon Kingdom of Two Sicilies. By early September, they had reached the Vallo di Diano and outskirts of Sala. Welcomed as a hero, Garibaldi dined with a leading citizen of Sala, Giuseppe De Petrinis, after the welcoming festivities ended.[2] As the weather worsened that evening, Garibaldi remained at the De Petrinis home before continuing to Naples the following morning.[3] Garibaldi's arrival and ensuing celebration must have impressed young Giovan. Over the next few years, news of Garibaldi's triumphs stirred his imagination, and surely planted a seed of hope that would help him escape a dismal future as a sharecropper or day laborer.

A few years later, according to another popular myth, fourteen-year-old Giovan left Sala to join Garibaldi's forces, purportedly serving as a drummer boy (*tamburino*). In 1866, thousands of volunteers across Italy answered Garibaldi's call to arms; their goal, the liberation of two northern Italian regions, Trentino and Veneto, from Austrian rule. Although the campaign was fought in the north, Garibaldi's fame and appeal drew willing men from all parts of Italy. By his fourteenth birthday, Giovan had matured enough to strike out on his own and his decision to join Garibaldi was logical for it provided him an opportunity to start his *own* life. As Garibaldi's volunteers passed through the Vallo di Diano, Giovan likely seized his chance and joined. Too young for combat, he served in some other capacity, very possibly as a drummer boy.

Giuseppe Garibaldi (1807-1882), Italian patriot and military hero. After returning to Italy from exile in 1848, Garibaldi and others battled for many years to achieve Italian unification. His success was acclaimed internationally and he was offered a command in the U.S. Army by Abraham Lincoln during the American Civil War (which he politely refused).

Martino proudly recounted marching with Garibaldi during interviews. He offered few details, however, and as the lone source, it may be impossible to substantiate his story while not entirely invalidating it. During a lengthy newspaper interview in 1906, Martino – his name had changed to Martin by this time – discussed the Little Bighorn and briefly touched on other parts of his life. As the interview progressed in Martino's Brooklyn apartment, he allowed the journalist to view a diary for the "… purpose of verifying the facts of his story."[4] Unfortunately, other than the inclusion of limited excerpts, the journalist offered few details on the diary itself. The narrative of the entries, as quoted within the article, hinted that the diary served more as a memoir, and less a daily record. It was written in English, which enabled the interviewer to read it sans translation. Martino's illiteracy prevented him from penning the diary while he lived in Italy and during his first years in America; although a precise date or period of its composition cannot be determined, the reporter noted that at the time of the interview – September 1906 – the 51-year-old Martin had made his final entry. From the limited excerpts, and when compared to other accounts, the diary appears detailed and mostly, but not entirely, factual. One of Martino's sons, George or

Frank, kept the diary following his father's death, but it was lost during a house fire many years ago.

The journalist repeated the claim that Martin joined Garibaldi as a drummer boy at the age of fourteen, and included a reference to the Battle of Villafranca. In 1922, an aging Martin was interviewed by Graham, who wrote, "[Martino] had enlisted with Garibaldi, as a drummer boy of fourteen, in the Army of Liberation, and had seen the backs of the Austrians at Villa Franca [sic] in '66."[5] Pasquale Petrocelli's study on the life of Martin correctly substituted Custoza in place of Villafranca.[6] On June 24, 1866, Austrian forces routed the Italian Army at the Battle of Custoza (near Verona), although the initial clash occurred on the heights near Villafranca. Garibaldi was not present at Custoza, however, and remained with his own forces near Brescia. If Martino fought at Custoza, it confirmed he made the long trip north, and that he was *not* marching with Garibaldi "as a drummer boy." Graham's words and Martino's diary – that he had "seen the backs of Austrians at Villa Franca" - appear inaccurate.

The diary added that Martino remained "… in the service four years [1866 through 1870] until that General's army was disbanded." Perhaps Martino never marched north, but instead volunteered for Garibaldi's march on Rome in 1867. As it gathered men from the south, this volunteer army may have attracted the attention of young Giovanni, especially as they neared his home in Sala. In 1870, another force of volunteers under the nominal leadership of Garibaldi advanced on Rome (before disbanding later that year), confirming the year referenced in Martino's diary entry. Neither Giovanni Martino nor Giovanni Martini appeared on the 'official' list of volunteers who served during the Garibaldi campaign of 1866, but this fact alone does not necessarily exclude him from having participated in some manner, possibly as the aforementioned drummer boy.[7] Most journalists, unaware of any dilemma, simply noted that Martin "fought with Garibaldi."

The most intriguing passage from the diary, as summarized by the reporter, noted that Martino enjoyed three peaceful years in Sala after returning from fighting with Garibaldi. In 1873, he was "… drafted into Victor Emanuel's army [ruler of the new Italian Republic], where he passed the examination, but was finally rejected because of the Italian conscription law which forbids the taking of an *only son* [author's italics] into the service." The surprising entry is unique for it marked the only reference of his familial position to appear in print. Its veracity is in question, yet certain details comport to actual events. Historically, conscription was required – and in effect in 1873 - for all males upon reaching their eighteenth birthday; all Italians men were required to provide a certificate indicating their military status before emigrating.[8] His 'only son' exemption released Martino from military service and he was free to leave Italy.

Was he the only son of Francesco and Mariantonia Botta? If he did not join the Italian Army (as he wrote), Francesco or Mariantonia Botta had to vouch before the military conscription board or civic officials that Giovan was indeed their only son. Perhaps they felt compelled to help Giovan after his many years of hard work (assuming he was not their only son). Sala's Civil records, though, would have indicated how many children were born to Francesco and Mariantonia Botta, and the falsehood easily discovered. Giovan's seemingly cryptic reference retained an element of truth, and for the second time, the answer lay within Sala's Civil Records. While researching the Registry of Births, Pasquale Petrocelli located an appendix that listed the names of Sala residents who had emigrated. He discovered a short transcription relating an interesting event: The Notary of Salerno, Giuseppe Arcieri de Sanza, recorded that a 50-year-old peasant named Giuseppe Perrone formally acknowledged Giovanni Martino as his son on October 24, 1872.[9] No reference to Giovan's birth mother appeared in the record.

The motivation for Perrone's admission remains a mystery, and he would not appear bound by any legal obligation. On further examination, Perrone may have acknowledged that Giovan was his only son so that the young man would be exempt from service and free to go abroad. Maybe a small payment by Giovan was part of an agreement; or, he may have cajoled his father to assist him. The foregoing scenario remains speculation with no direct proof to substantiate or refute it. Perhaps Giovan was aware that Perrone had fathered him, yet he did not assume the Perrone surname and continued to list Francesco and Mariantonia Botta as his parents on each of his Army re-enlistment documents.[10] The emotional impact to Giovan is unknown; perhaps his reticence signaled his sentiment on the matter. The stigma of being a foundling remained a secret Martin carried all his life. Unfortunately, the indifference of journalists on the subject creates an abundance of questions and possibilities. The journalist concluded the passage with a disappointed Martino expressing his "… failure to get into the fray once more …" and leaving for America to join the cavalry.[11]

Regardless of his exact circumstances, a young and energetic Giovanni must have grown restless with Sala and the prospect of a life as a *contadino*. Marching with Garibaldi had given him a taste of adventure and a world beyond the valleys and farms of Sala. Seeking a new life, Martino embarked for America in March 1873. The nascent Italian government encouraged emigration, hoping to relieve some of its economic burden.

Joined by fellow immigrants from Sala bound for America, Giovanni Martino made his way to Naples and boarded the Anchor Line's S.S. Tyrian in late March 1873. They were fortunate to have traveled only to Naples; during this period preceding the great rush of Italian immigration, most of the shipping companies carrying passengers to America rarely docked in Italian ports. In 1873, American-bound passenger lines infrequently sailed into the Mediterranean and preferred to conduct their business at the more profitable Atlantic ports.[12]

The S.S. Tyrian, a relatively new vessel, was rigged for sailing. The immigration manifest indicates the Tyrian carried approximately 667 passengers during its trip across the Atlantic Ocean in late March 1873. Following brief stops in Marseilles and Glasgow, the Tyrian reached New York after twenty-seven long days at sea. After paying a fee of $15, he joined other steerage passengers berthed below deck in "communal open sleeping quarters." The discomfort knew no bounds and "primitive sanitary conditions, seasickness and over-crowding transformed steerage into a horrid place."[13]

The Anchor Line's S.S. Tyrian.

After passing a quarantine inspection in New York Harbor, the Tyrian's immigrant passengers were transported by smaller vessels to a Manhattan pier and disembarked. They were separated by gender and "... marched into the castle for medical examinations."[14] The castle referred to New York State's immigration processing facility in lower Manhattan, Castle Garden (now Castle Clinton). Martino and other immigrants were led into the Castle's rotunda room and seated on wooden benches as they awaited their turn to be processed by a staff of nearly one hundred Registering Department clerks representing various State agencies.[15] One by one, the weary immigrants were ushered to clerks, according to their language, and interviewed, with their vital data logged into an immigration manifest.[16] Once he completed the registration process at Castle Garden, Giovanni Martino crossed the East River into Brooklyn, a New York City borough filled with recently immigrated southern Italians. Martino's registration signaled a new phase in his life, but the "Americanization" of his name – Giovanni Martino to John Martin – did not occur at this time.

Part II

The Middle Years

CHAPTER FIVE

Bugler Martin

A few months after Martino's arrival, a severe national recession – the Panic of 1873 – swept across the United States. In the years following the Civil War, the American economy rapidly expanded: "Prosperity was written all over the face of things. Manufacturers were busy, workmen in demand ... Prices of commodities were high, demand pretty good. Everybody seemed to be making money ..."[1] Speculators ignored warning signs, and continued to pour millions of dollars into unsound investments. The failure of the Northern Pacific Railroad's principal backer, Jay Cooke & Company, signaled the beginning of the Panic in mid-September 1873. As the nation's leading investment firm, Jay Cooke's collapse initiated financial calamity on an epic level:[2] Credit vanished while banks and factories closed their doors. In a very short time, perhaps one third of working Americans were jobless.[3] Even Nature conspired to deepen their misery as grasshopper plagues destroyed many crops. Five long years passed before the economy recovered.

The Panic notwithstanding, immigrants had few employment opportunities in the late nineteenth century.[4] They faced many difficulties in their new country, beginning with language barriers that slowed assimilation into American culture. Xenophobic fears emerged as Americans preferred immigrants of similar ethnic and religious backgrounds as their own.[5] Southern Italians were especially punished for their rampant illiteracy, and relegated to menial work for meager pay.[6] The long hours for substandard wages ensured the cycle of poverty would continue. With luck and determination, unmarried men might accumulate enough money to find better housing and clothing, but laborers with families were very limited, and their wages were quickly consumed by the high cost of housing and food. Opportunities were marginally better in larger cities like New York, Chicago and San Francisco where construction projects created an abundance of jobs. Although the wages were relatively high, the cost of living in urban centers leveled out most of their gains.[7] Immigrants often faced a new version of the same limitations they escaped, and some chose to return to their homelands. Most, however, could not afford the trip home and decided to remain.

Seeking an alternative to unemployment or menial labor, many men turned to the United States Army. Economic depressions, and the resulting high rate of unemployment, tend to swell Army enrollments and the Panic of 1873 was no different. Army pay was low but guaranteed as was room, board and clothing.[8] Italy endured decades of intermittent war during its three wars for Unification; the nearly constant strife produced battle-hardened men anxious to prove their worth and earn a living in their new country. For Martino, the grinding routine of wage labor must have paled in comparison to his experiences with Garibaldi. As he passed an Army enlistment center in New York one day, recruiter Lieutenant Edward Hunter approached Martino with promises of a steady job and a good wage.[9] With few options available, he enlisted on June 1, 1874 and received an assignment as a trumpeter to Company H of the U.S. Army's Seventh Cavalry Regiment. Reflecting his new life in a new country, Giovanni Martino's new "American" name - John Martin - appeared for the first time in his enlistment documents, as did a physical description of the twenty-one year old: 5'6" in height with brown eyes, black hair, and a dark complexion.

An undated photograph of a young John Martin (Giovanni Martino). Despite the photograph's poor quality, it appears to date to his arrival in 1873 to the United States.

Mirroring an increasingly diversified American population, the Seventh Cavalry Regiment was comprised of nearly equal parts foreign and American-born troopers.[10] The majority of foreign-born troopers hailed from Ireland and Germany, augmented by a mix of other nationalities. Martin was joined by five other Italian-born troopers in the Seventh, all of whom also anglicized (or "Americanized") their names at varying levels prior to enlistment: Private John James (born Giovanni Casella); Private Augustus De Voto (Augusto De Voto); Private Frank Lombard or Lombardy (Francesco Lombardi); First Lieutenant Charles Camillus DeRudio (Carlo Camillo Di Rudio); and, Felix Vinatieri (Felice Villiet Vinatieri), the diminutive leader of Custer's Seventh Cavalry band.[11]

Martin was sent to the Army's recruiting depot at Jefferson Barracks, Missouri, to begin his training. The average age for most first-time enlistments was 23 years (the minimum age was 21). Each man signed on for five years and received $13 per month, before deductions.[12] Most were illiterate, like Martin; accordingly, no written manuals existed and training was conducted primarily in the field through verbal instructions. Standard-issue Army uniforms included a dark blue wool waist jacket, with brass buttons and yellow rank stripes, blue flannel shirt, light blue trousers, boots and a wide-rimmed felt hat. Barracks were crowded and mostly devoid of hygienic safeguards. Privacy was a privilege reserved for Sergeants, who slept in separate small rooms while corporals and privates shared the open barrack. The troopers survived on a steady diet of salt pork, stew, beans, hardtack crackers, vinegar, molasses and strong coffee; wild game, hunted near the post, augmented their meals occasionally.[13]

All daily activity at Jefferson Barracks, from early morning until evening, was structured and regulated according to a rigidly observed schedule. In the absence of clocks, an array of bugle calls signaled the start of each activity, beginning with Reveille call at 6:00 a.m. After breakfast, a bugle call sent troopers to work details and then to their morning drills; following a break for the midday meal, bugle calls announced further drills and work details that continued throughout the afternoon. At 9:00 p.m., Evening "Tattoo" was sounded, followed soon after by the final call of the day, "Taps."

Under the auspices of noncommissioned Officers, most of whom were combat-experienced Civil War veterans, Martin received formal military training.[14] Officers had to work quickly and "... recruits received only the most basic instruction during their short time at Jefferson Barracks."[15] Developing the necessary skills required time, but the Army was short on soldiers and their training was abbreviated. Recruits concentrated primarily on basic horsemanship skills, including mounting and dismounting, riding in formation, and firing a weapon while mounted.[16] They were armed with Colt Single Action Army .45 caliber revolvers and single-shot .45 caliber Springfield rifles. Marksmanship drills were very limited with troopers issued only fifteen rounds of ammunition per month "allotted for target practice (just increased from ten rounds the previous September), which was highly irregular at best ..."[17] Success in battle would be achieved by the troopers' concentrated and coordinated fire – however poorly aimed - rather than an individual's skill with a firearm.

Martin's Army enlistment papers listed his former occupation as musician. Whether he was proficient with any instrument other than the drum is unknown, but his assigned duty as a company trumpeter in the Seventh Regiment was predictable. One aspect of the period's prevalent Italian stereotype included a superior musical ability (as compared to other immigrant groups). Of the six Italians in the Seventh Regiment, half served in a musically related capacity: Chief Musician Felix Vinatieri as regimental bandmaster; Frank Lombard, also a band member (instrument unknown); and. John Martin, trumpeter. To perform his duties, he was issued the standard U.S. Army Cavalry bugle; the two-loop brass instrument was approximately seventeen inches long and remained at Martin's side throughout his thirty years of military service. Once he mastered the fundamentals of playing a bugle, the next phase of training required memorization of nearly one hundred different bugle calls. With the Army's shortened training schedule, Martin had to learn quickly.

On campaigns, Army trumpeters also performed the duties of orderlies or messengers; each company was assigned two trumpeters to ensure one remained available at all times. Tasked with shuttling written and verbal orders between commands, orderlies had to "demonstrate the ability to repeat a twenty-word order verbatim."[18] Their individual ability to memorize *and* speak English was tested. Three years later, Martin's qualification as an orderly would be a key component in the events - and controversies – at the Little Bighorn.

In less than a month, with his training completed, Trooper John Martin reported for duty with the Seventh Cavalry Regiment at their base, Fort Abraham Lincoln (located near present-day Bismarck, North Dakota). For the first time in ten years, the 12 companies that comprised the Seventh Cavalry gathered at Fort Lincoln in preparation for their upcoming expedition into the Black Hills (Dakota Territory): At full strength, the Seventh Regiment totaled nearly 800 enlisted men and forty-three officers, all under the command of General Custer.

While preferable to poverty, Cavalry life was difficult and deadly work. Hard labor, poor sanitation, and a generally low quality diet not only added to the troopers' misery, but also threatened their lives. Most camps and forts were deficient when it came to proper medical care; soldiers with a modicum of education or previous medical experience were often pressed into service as medical officers. Ultimately, any one of the many diseases that ravaged frontier posts took more lives than actual battles or campaigns.[19] If cholera or dysentery failed to down a trooper, he might succumb to alcoholism, a consequence of the endless tedium endured in outpost duty on the Plains. Post traders (or sutlers) operated stores near established camps and forts, from which they peddled goods like tobacco and clothing; sutlers also sold beer and wine to off-duty troopers.[20] If the troopers' hard-earned wages were not exhausted from purchasing liquor, they sought pleasure from one of the "professional ladies" that worked at a nearby bawdy house, less beautifully referred to as a "hog ranch."[21]

CHAPTER SIX

Custer and the Indians

At the urging of U.S. Interior Secretary Columbus Delano, Brigadier General Alfred H. Terry formally ordered an expedition into the Black Hills (Dakota Territory) in June 1874. Persistent reports claimed the Hills were home to a bounty of untapped mineral resources, perhaps even gold, but the Black Hills - sacred land to the American Indians - were protected by the Fort Laramie Treaty of 1868, which guaranteed ownership to the Lakota nation. With Lieutenant Colonel George A. Custer in command, the large expedition included ten companies of his Seventh Cavalry Regiment, two companies of infantry, scouts, guides, newspaper correspondents, photographers, miners and scientists. On July 2, 1874, as they lumbered out of Fort Abraham Lincoln (Dakota Territory), Martin rode with his new unit, Company H. After nearly sixty days and 1,200 miles, the expedition returned to their base at Fort Lincoln on August 30. Their success, transmitted by telegraph lines, preceded their return.

Newspaper headlines screamed the news across the country: Gold had been discovered in the Black Hills! Prospectors and speculators rushed to the territory hoping to strike it rich. The Lakota (Sioux) and other Indian tribes protested vehemently to the U.S. Government about the incursions onto their sacred land. In response, the Army was ordered to remove the trespassers, but the task proved too difficult and they were unable to enforce the removal policy effectively.

After the Lakota rejected a series of offers to sell the Black Hills, the U.S. Government issued an ultimatum: All tribes had to relocate to designated reservations by the end of January 1876. Little consideration was given to understanding the Plains Indians, composed primarily of Lakota (Sioux), Arapaho, and Cheyenne, along with contingents of Kiowas and Comanches. While many resigned themselves to a life on the government reservations, others were outraged by the continued incursions onto their sacred lands. Encouraged by Hunkpapa (Lakota) holy man and spiritual leader, Sitting Bull, the "hostile" tribes were determined to resist and refused to move to the reservations as ordered. For their common defense, the assorted tribes united in an immense camp "... that strung along the Little Bighorn River for a distance of nearly four miles" and totaled perhaps ten thousand men, women and children by some estimates. Any calculations on the true size of the Indian village are speculative; Army and Indian accounts varied widely on the total numbers. By most estimates, however, after subtracting non-combatants, approximately 4,000 resolute warriors prepared to defend their families and way of life.[1]

Enforcement of the ultimatum fell to the Army and General Alfred Terry planned a winter offensive, but delays postponed the start until the early spring. Three independent columns of cavalry and infantry mobilized from their winter camps and planned to rendezvous in the vicinity of the Yellowstone River. The combined force would locate and envelop the Indian camp - its exact location still unknown - to force them back to the reservations. Accordingly, Colonel John Gibbon led the first column of 500 men out of Fort Ellis (Montana territory) on March 30 to patrol the west side of the Yellowstone River valley. A second force deployed from Fort Fetterman (Wyoming territory) on May 29 under General George Crook, and his command of over 1,300 men marched northeast.

The Seventh Cavalry Regiment, approximately 700 troopers, formed the third element and they rode north under the command of Civil War hero, Lieutenant Colonel George Armstrong Custer. He exemplified the ideal of the romantic *beau sabreur*; Custer was "the army's best-known – and, to many Americans of the time, best – Indian fighter."[2] Born in 1839 in Rumley, Ohio, Custer attended the U.S. Military Academy at West Point in New York. He graduated in 1861 albeit ranked last in his class of 34 cadets. With the onset of the American Civil War, Union forces desperately needed trained officers; immediately upon graduation, and despite his poor academic record, Custer was rushed to the front lines. He served with distinction throughout the war, from the first Battle of Bull Run to the final campaign and surrender at Appomattox. His aggressive cavalry tactics produced positive results, often at a high cost in men and horses. When the war ended in 1865, Custer held a brevet (or temporary) rank of Brigadier General, but reverted to Captain the following year. By 1868, he received a promotion to Lieutenant Colonel; protocol required him to sign and be addressed by his brevet rank of

Major General. Impetuous, courageous and sometimes reckless, Custer sought glory and a quick end to the Indian problem. He excelled at managing his public image and while some of his reputation as an Indian fighter was self-generated propaganda, he lacked neither experience nor courage. High public office was not out of the question had he survived the Little Bighorn.

Lieutenant Colonel George A. Custer in a photograph dating to the American Civil War. Custer, two of his brothers, a cousin, and brother-in-law were killed during the fight at the Little Big Horn. Custer's body was reinterred at West Point in October 1877.

(Courtesy Library of Congress: Prints and Photographs Division)
(Call number: LC-BH831- 1314)

One of Custer's earliest encounters with Indian warriors came in late November 1868. Ordered to locate and destroy hostile tribes in the vicinity of the Washita River (Oklahoma), Custer's Seventh Cavalry Regiment surrounded and attacked Chief Black Kettle's camp of southern Cheyenne Indians. Unprepared and poorly armed, the Indians were cut down and the bloody snow covered with the bodies of over one hundred dead warriors, women and children; what remained was burned to the ground and hundreds of ponies - crucial for the survival of nomadic tribes like the Cheyenne - were slaughtered. It marked the beginning of a new phase in the western theatre, the strategy of total war, and an experienced commander like Custer was willing to execute it. At Washita, striking quickly and decisively proved successful for Custer and he would employ the same tactics at the Little Bighorn, but with tragically different results.

CHAPTER SEVEN

The Campaign

"We are at Fort Abraham Lincoln, Dakota Territory," announced Martin's diary, "it was the first time in years that Seventh Cavalry had been united." In the spring of 1876, the Seventh Cavalry's companies were recalled to Fort Lincoln after serving the previous eighteen months in constabulary duty in outposts scattered throughout Texas and the southwest; John Martin's Company H quartered in New Orleans. Custer finally arrived at Fort Lincoln in mid-May following a politically charged dispute that delayed him in Washington, D.C. Martin recalled, "... [Custer] did not have much to say, for at that time, he was in trouble with General (President) Grant. But he had the spirit."[1] General Custer found the Seventh unprepared for the campaign: Training had been lax and horsemanship skills for the many new recruits remained poor; riders unable to control their mounts - or even tend to their horse's health - posed a danger to the trooper and his comrades.

Cold and fog greeted the troopers in the early morning hours of Wednesday, May 17, 1876. Reveille sounded at 4:00 a.m., but a heavy mist prevented any fires for coffee and added to the general misery. "The troops for this expedition," the diary detailed, "consisted of twelve troops of the Seventh Cavalry, four companies of infantry, ten of fifteen Indian scouts, and twenty-five or thirty civilians [approximately 750 men]."[2] Hoping to advance quickly, Custer eschewed the use of slow-moving wagons, and instead opted for a large mule train (or pack train) to carry ammunition and other supplies.

By 6:30 a.m., as the weather cleared, the mounted troopers lined up by company in columns of four and rode slowly through the fort while the regimental band played. Custer's wife, Elizabeth (Libbie), accompanied her husband and described the emotional departure, "After we had passed the Indian Quarters we came near Laundress Row, and there my heart entirely failed me. The wives of children of the soldiers lined the road. Mothers, with streaming eyes, held their little ones out at arm's length for one last look at the departing father. The toddlers among the children ... made a mimic column of their own. They were too young to realize why the mothers wailed out their farewells."[3] Captain Thomas Custer, the General's brother, halted the command outside of the fort and ordered officers and married men to "dismount and fall out," thus allowing them a brief, and for many, final goodbye. Martin's diary added, "Then we passed in review and bade farewell to our friends and though the band was playing 'The Girl I Left Behind Me,' it seemed like a funeral procession." As the column rode off, many of the troopers in tears, Martin recalled the band played "Custer's favorite tune, 'Garrion' [Garry Owen or Garryowen]."[4]

Martin's diary detailed the order of march, "General Terry and staff in front, followed by General Custer and staff (Mrs. Custer rode on the left of the General)." As she often did, Libbie Custer rode out with the command, a privilege accorded only to her. By the end of the day, "we made Little Heart River [roughly thirteen miles from Fort Lincoln] and camped for the night. After pitching camp assembly was sounded (I was a bugler) and we fell in for payment." In an effort to stop troopers from squandering their money, General Terry ordered their wages distributed far from the temptations of liquor and 'hog ranches' by Fort Lincoln. The uncertainty of the campaign weighed on all. "It was a pretty sober crowd," Martin commented, "everybody felt the position we were in." On the following morning, after a short delay, the march resumed. "Poor Mrs. Custer went back to Fort Abraham Lincoln," began a melancholy entry in Martin's diary, "... it proved to be the last farewell for her and the General."[5] As Custer and a company of troopers scouted in advance of the main column, the late start limited their march to eleven miles. Heavy rain battered them throughout 14 long miles on the following day.

Each day brought more riding and by May 26, the command had traveled nearly one hundred miles over hard terrain: "A rough, broken country of considerable elevation," described Lieutenant Edward S. Godfrey, an officer with the Seventh, "high precipitous hills and deep, narrow gulches."[6] The early part of the campaign became routine. Martin and the other company buglers sounded Reveille, usually at 4:20 a.m., and while troopers readied their horses for the day's march, company cooks prepared a breakfast of hard bread, bacon and strong coffee. "Several days of dreary, heart-breaking marches are recorded," the reporter summarized from Martin's diary, "with a hot sun and dusty plains as constant sources of discomfort to the men."[7] In the evenings, after tending to their mounts and eating, the tired troopers "grouped about the fires and sang songs and spun yarns until 'taps.'"[8] Tempers flared during the march and Martin described one particular incident with Henry Voss, the Regiment's Chief Trumpeter. On May 29, as they camped by the Little Missouri River, Voss "... detailed me as mounted orderly for headquarters; but as it was not my turn, I refused to do the duty, and after some words the chief trumpeter had me tied up on the picket line for two hours (strung up by the thumbs)." An upset Martin spoke to his company commander, Captain Frederick Benteen, who reported the matter to General Custer. "[Custer] sent for me," Martin wrote, "and said he would have it investigated as soon as we got back to quarters."[9] Martin's assignment to accompany Custer's headquarters staff was routine and part of a rotation among all of the company buglers. Reasons for his displeasure with the order are unrecorded, but one possibility may be that, as a trumpeter, Martin found orderly duty beneath him.

On the following day, they crossed the Little Missouri and went eleven miles before making camp. That night, the rain turned to snow as the temperature dropped and delayed the march for two days, as troopers, horses and mules suffered from the cold. The Regiment moved out once more on June 3, and encountered scouts from Colonel Gibbon's column before camping by Beaver Creek. Sixty more miles were covered over the next three days; on June 7, as rain pelted the troopers, they managed to slog through thirty-two hard miles. In three weeks, the command had traveled nearly 300 miles over hard ground, with only a few days of rest. Exhaustion started taking a toll on the men, yet only six troopers deserted during the march.

On June 22, scouts finally located a large fresh Indian trail leading to the Little Bighorn Valley. Terry immediately ordered Custer and the Seventh to follow it. The command arose and mounted without the usual bugle calls on June 23. The command had advanced quietly for two days and "every precaution had been taken to conceal our march."[10] Custer ordered "Trumpet calls would not be sounded except in an emergency." The Seventh rode thirty-three hard miles that day, followed by another 28 miles on June 24, and "passed through many Indian camping places."[11] The camps were recently vacated, and confirmed for Custer that they were on the right trail. As the weary troopers settled down late that night, a scout rode in and reported "the discovery of a large fresh camp" by the Little Bighorn River (in present-day Montana). In the early morning hours of June 25, Custer, a scout named Mitch Bouyer (or Boyer), and assorted other officers and scouts climbed a small hill to view the Indian village a few miles away. Despite the use of field glasses and the scouts' insistence, Custer failed to see it clearly in the morning haze. In exasperation, Bouyer purportedly told Custer, "Well, General, if you don't find more Indians in that valley than you ever saw together, you can hang me."[12]

CHAPTER EIGHT

Cooke's Message

A little before 8:00 a.m. on June 25, "Trumpeter Vose [Voss] called back to me to report as orderly to General Custer," the diary related, "although, again, it was not my turn, [but] I did as he commanded." Martin's recollection is imprecise: He told Graham in 1922 that Benteen ordered him to report to Custer, yet his diary – written no later than 1906 – indicated Chief Trumpeter Voss issued the order. As troopers prepared their mounts, Martin reported to Custer who "just looked at me and nodded."[1] With a battle imminent, and the need to maintain constant communication between units, Martin was one of several orderlies attached to the headquarters staff that day. On that morning, Custer was wearing "a blue-gray flannel shirt, buckskin trousers and long boots," and his distinctive "yellow hair was cut short," Martin recalled for Graham, "not very short - but it was not long and curly on his shoulders like it used to be."[2] Martin sat down a few feet away from Custer as the General spoke with an Indian scout named Bloody Knife. Through an interpreter, Bloody Knife appeared to be telling Custer of a "big village in the valley, several hundred tepees and about five thousand Sioux."[3]

Promptly at 8:00 a.m., the command set off towards the Indian village. The men grew anxious as scouts raced ahead of the column, then returned to speak with Custer. "We knew, of course, that plenty of Indians were somewhere near," Martin explained, "because we had been going through deserted villages for two days."[4] Later that morning, scouts reported that small parties of Indians had spotted their column. The news vexed Custer as it eliminated the crucial element of surprise.

Fearless yet prudent warriors, Indians preferred to fight when conditions assured success; if they perceived any disadvantage in an upcoming battle, warriors often chose to flee, especially when their families were threatened. Tribes were limited in resources, and warriors not easily replaced; substantial losses in battle – including horses and ponies - were unacceptable if the tribe expected to survive. The Army, however, possessed a seemingly infinite supply of men and materials, yet logistical issues remained a concern. Army columns lacked the speed and mobility of warrior combatants. To handle the 'Indian problem' on the Plains, the Army relied on an operational doctrine of surprise and superior forces; a strategy designed to reduce long expensive campaigns that wore down men, animals and equipment. At Washita, Custer executed the doctrine perfectly as the Seventh's three assault columns approached the camp unnoticed, then surrounded and overwhelmed Black Kettle's camp.[5]

Neglecting his general orders to wait for the other columns, and severely underestimating the Indian warriors' numerical superiority and resolve, Custer opted to attack immediately. The sheer size of the village and number of warriors was unfathomable to Custer who had yet to see the entire village. He believed the order and discipline of his Seventh effectively eliminated numerical advantages. With the village nearby and battle imminent, Custer "ordered me to sound officers' call and I did so," Martin said, "… there was no use to keep quiet any longer."[6] Following the late morning meeting with his officers, Custer divided the 700 troopers of the Seventh into three attack battalions, just as he had at Washita.

After the troopers mounted, the Seventh "… moved out in column of fours, fifty feet between each company." Leading the way was Custer, followed closely by his adjutant, "the drundreary-whiskered" Lieutenant William W. Cooke; two color-bearers, Chief Trumpeter Voss and Martin trailed directly behind Cooke.[7] After several miles, Major Marcus A. Reno and three companies (around 140 troopers) were ordered to "… march down the Little Big Horn valley and charge everything before him …"[8] Benteen, also in command of three companies, was sent to the southwest to block any escape. Captain Thomas McDougall and one company rode with the Regiment's pack train of mules laden with ammunition and supplies.

"We went at a gallop," Martin recounted for Graham, "The General seemed to be in a big hurry." Custer and five companies (approximately 220 troopers) rode for one or two miles, by Martin's estimate, before arriving at "… a big hill that overlooked the valley." The command halted near its base while Custer, Martin and the headquarters staff climbed the hill (or ridge) for their first look at the Indian encampment across the river. "It was a big village, but we couldn't see it all from there, though we didn't know it then," Martin recalled, "but several hundred tepees were in plain sight."[9] Martin told Camp in 1908 that as Custer and his officers viewed the village through field glasses, they observed "… children and dogs playing among the tepees but no warriors or horses except a few loose ponies grazing around." The General, Martin recalled, "… seemed both surprised and glad …" by what he saw, and the officers debated whether the warriors were away hunting buffalo or still asleep in their tents.[10] Both interpretations proved erroneous: While some of the warriors had gone to address the threat posed by Reno's advance, many others had raced to their horses and ponies fully intending to fight.

Custer "turned in the saddle and took off his hat and waved it so the men of the command …" waiting at the base of the hill, Martin recounted. In his high-pitched voice, the General shouted, "Hurrah, boys, we've got them! We'll finish them up and then go home to our station."[11] The troopers answered with three cheers. Martin's diary reflected a slightly different speech, with Custer exhorting, "Boys, have courage! Be brave, and as soon as we get through with these Indians we will go home to our winter station."[12] In other eyewitness accounts, Custer and Cooke waved their hats to Reno's men who were beginning their attack on the valley floor before the General addressed his men.

After he rejoined the troops, Custer and his experienced adjutant, Lieutenant Cooke, conferred briefly. Following a mile of hard riding, the command reached a deep ravine that led down to the Little Bighorn and the village. While the exact time remains in dispute, it was probably around 3:35 p.m., and just moments before Custer launched his attack. As the men started to descend into the ravine, Custer called Martin over. "Orderly, I want you to take a message to Benteen. Ride as fast as you can and tell him to hurry," the General's words tumbled out rapidly, "Tell him it's a big village and I want him to be quick, and to bring the ammunition packs [boxes]." Martin did not reply verbally, but only nodded and checked his horse. Lieutenant Cooke called out, "Wait, orderly." As he pulled a field order pad from his jacket, Cooke told Martin, "I'll give you a message."[13] Cooke noticed how quickly the excited Custer spoke and perhaps doubted Martin's ability to comprehend the order clearly and precisely. Echoing Custer's orders, Cooke's note read:

Benteen
Come on. Big Village.
Be quick. Bring packs.

W. W. Cooke

P.S. Bring Pacs.

The packs – hastily misspelled as 'pacs' – referred to the ammunition boxes carried by the mule train. Although Benteen and others offered conflicting interpretations of the message, its urgency was unmistakable: "Be quick. Bring packs."

As he handed the dispatch to Martin, Cooke instructed, "Now, orderly, ride as fast as you can to Benteen. Take the same trail we came down. If you have time and there is no danger, come back; but otherwise stay with your company."[14] Cooke's specific commands stressed the immediate need for Benteen to support Custer's attack. Martin's diary, however, described a different scenario. Custer perused the note, which had already been written, before calling for an orderly to deliver it. An unidentified trooper, likely another orderly, stepped out to which Custer replied, "No, no, the other man [Martin]." As Martin took the dispatch, Custer instructed, "Trumpeter, go back on our trail and see if you can discover Benteen and give him this message. If you see no danger come back to us, but if you find Indians in your way stay with Benteen and return with him and when you get back to us report."[15]

In 1879, the Army convened a Court of Inquiry at the insistence of Major Reno, Custer's second in command at the Little Bighorn; Reno hoped to clear his name following questionable conduct – including allegations of drunkenness - during the battle. Martin testified at the Inquiry that as Custer started to lead his men down a ravine towards the river, the General told Cooke to send a message to Benteen. Martin, almost directly behind Custer at the time, was taken aside by Cooke who rapidly scribbled the written order, and instructed, "Orderly, I want you to take this despatch (sic) to Captain Benteen and go as fast as you can." Cooke continued, "If you have time and there is no danger, come back and report to me, but if there are any Indians in the way, stay with Captain Benteen's company." He repeated this version to Walter Mason Camp in 1910.[16]

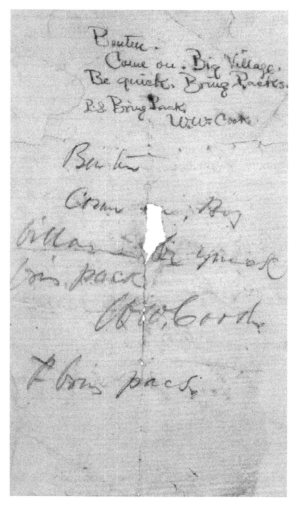

Custer's last order, handwritten by Lieutenant William W. Cooke, was carried by John Martin to Captain Frederick Benteen just before the attack began. The original note is written in the center of the page; it was rewritten at the top by Benteen for legibility. The dispatch was finally located by Colonel William A. Graham and donated to the Army through the efforts of Colonel Charles Bates. It resides in the library at the U.S. Military Academy at West Point.

(Courtesy of the West Point Museum Art Collection, United States Military Academy, West Point, New York.)

The exchanges between Martin, Cooke and Custer raise two key issues: Martin's recollection of the events and Cooke's motivation for writing the order. Over the course of his life, Martin's account of the moments leading up to Custer's attack appeared in print many times. The most prominent and detailed narrations were his two interviews with Walter Mason Camp (1908 and 1910), a series of three interviews with Colonel William A. Graham in 1922, a newspaper article that quoted from Martin's diary (1906), and the 1879 Court of Inquiry testimony. In three of the dialogues, Martin stated he spoke directly with Custer.[17] He omitted his conversation with Custer at the Court of Inquiry and in his second Camp interview in 1910. The conflicting renditions cast doubts about Martin's veracity, yet the differences are mostly trivial. Martin's advanced age (70 years old) during the last series of interviews with Graham contributed to some mistakes. Inaccuracies caused by Martin's imperfect English - less likely in 1922 than 1879 or 1908 - merits consideration. On a more personal level, Martin may have embellished his account, exaggerating to include a direct conversation with Custer, a man he idolized.

A few minutes earlier, Sergeant Daniel Kanipe of Company C rode off to find Benteen with a verbal order very similar to Martin's "Come Quick. Big Village." dispatch. Kanipe was sent to Benteen by Captain Tom Custer, the General's brother, after being directed to do so by Cooke. If Custer verbalized his order to Martin then turned to Cooke to write it down for the bugler, it would have embarrassed Martin who may have believed his proficiency in English neither warranted nor required a written order.

Cooke's intention or purpose in writing the order implied problems with Martin's ability to understand English. Martin was not normally assigned to Custer's headquarters staff and while the Lieutenant's unfamiliarity with him may have affected their communication, the core issue is whether the Army allowed a trooper with poor command of the language to serve as a trumpeter/orderly. After he completed his training as an orderly, Martin had to pass a proficiency test regarding his ability to hear and repeat orders. It must be assumed that Martin passed the exam and thus deemed capable of performing orderly duty. Were Martin incapable of speaking passable English, the Army would have assigned him to another duty. Too many lives would be jeopardized in allowing a trooper deficient in English to serve as an orderly.

CHAPTER NINE

Riding to Benteen

With the dispatch tucked away, Martin rode swiftly up the trail. "My horse was pretty tired, but I started back as fast as I could go," he told Graham, "It was a very warm day [but] I kept on as fast as I could go."[1] When he reached the crest of a succeeding ridge, Martin looked back in time to see "... the Indians had already attacked, and our boys were acting very excitedly." Back on the trail, Martin spotted a solitary rider headed in his direction. It was General Custer's younger brother, Boston, a civilian who accompanied the regiment as a guide and forager. Boston had been with McDougall's pack (mule) train but when Sergeant Kanipe arrived with a request to "hurry up" the ammunition, he immediately rode to Custer's command. Where's the General, Boston shouted as he reined in his horse. Martin pointed and replied, "Right behind that next ridge you'll find him."[2] Young Boston spurred his horse and disappeared over the ridge. Five members of the Custer family perished that afternoon.[3] Ironically, if this brief meeting occurred, it united the last trooper to see Custer alive and the last man to join the doomed column.

Martin heard several shots from his left, he remembered, "but I was lucky and did not get hit." He was unaware that his horse had been struck in the hip several times, and that its blood had splattered onto his back. In 1922, he told Graham that Benteen pointed out the horse's wounds after Martin delivered the dispatch.[4] In the 1908 interview with Camp, however, Martin said his horse was hit before he encountered Boston Custer, and that Boston brought his attention to the bullet wounds.

Martin followed the trail back and finally located Benteen around 4:00 p.m. A relieved Martin trotted up - his wounded horse could go no faster - saluted and handed the dispatch to Benteen. "I told him what the General said," Martin recalled, "that it was a big village and to hurry."[5] Martin omitted the "big village" comment in another version.[6] Benteen read the message, and asked for Custer's location. In his diary and Graham interview, Martin indicated he replied, "About 3 miles from here."

"Is Custer being attacked or not?" snapped Benteen.

"Yes, [he] is being attacked," Martin answered.[7] In 1922, Martin told Graham that he recalled telling Benteen, "… the Indians we saw were running and I supposed that by this time he had charged through the village."[8] During the Court of Inquiry in 1879, Benteen testified, "[Martin] said the Indians were all skedaddling, therefore there was less necessity for me going back to the packs." In the three-year period between the battle and Court of Inquiry, questions emerged regarding Benteen's slow response to Custer's last message. The Captain's contempt for Custer was common knowledge within the regiment, and when reports of their discord reached the public, Benteen's actions after receiving the dispatch were scrutinized.

Martin denied using any form of the word 'skedaddle' - Army slang for retreating or running away - during one of the Camp interviews,[9] and did not even mention the matter in his diary or during the Graham interviews. Martin may have repeated an interpretation of Custer's words to Benteen, perhaps reflecting the General's initial reaction to a mostly empty village. Benteen himself may have interpreted Martin's reply as the equivalent of 'skedaddle.' Although Martin never confessed to having said 'skedaddle,' he inferred it by any accepted definition of the word in his admission to Graham that, "… the Indians we saw were running." As the officer in charge of three companies, Benteen was required to "inquire into the matter until he was satisfied," yet the Captain failed to do so.[10]

In a private letter written to his wife one week after the battle, Benteen placed blame for the disastrous outcome on Custer: It was the Boy General, Benteen wrote, who "… disobeyed orders from the fact of not wanting any other command -- or body to have a finger in the pie - and thereby lost his life."[11] In the same letter, Benteen did not mention any problems communicating with Martin. He noted only that the bugler's life was saved by delivering the message and that Martin told him Custer's men were cheering loudly as they dropped down into the ravine.[12] By 1879, however, casting Custer as the scapegoat proved ineffective while the foreign-born Martin presented an easier, if not more convenient target. It was a habit of Benteen to assign others culpability for his own misdoings.

Captain Frederick W. Benteen in a photograph by David F. Barry. Born in 1834, he served with the Union Army during the Civil War and remained an Army officer for 27 years. After receiving Custer's note from Martin, Benteen and his command united with Major Reno's remaining troopers and fought off Indian attacks for two days before their rescue by General Terry's relief column. Benteen disliked Custer since their first meeting in 1867, finding the General "vain, arrogant and egotistical."

At the Court of Inquiry, Second Lieutenant Winfield Edgerly testified that after delivering the dispatch to Benteen, Martin joyfully remarked to the Captain's orderly (possibly the other Company H trumpeter, William Ramell) that it was the "... biggest village he [Martin] ever saw," and added that Major Reno's battalion "was charging it and killing everything - men, women and children." Edgerly said he *assumed* Benteen heard this conversation, yet Benteen neglected to mention it during his detailed testimony, although it would have reinforced his earlier assertion that Martin used the word 'skedaddle' when he returned with the message.[13] Other than Edgerly's testimony, this incident is not acknowledged by anyone else who testified during the Court of Inquiry; one example of the many discrepancies glossed over during the Inquiry.

When Sergeant Kanipe delivered Custer's first message to Benteen, the Sergeant was ordered to ride back and hurry forward the slow moving pack train. As Kanipe rode past Benteen's Company, he shouted, "We've got them, boys!"[14] In the ensuing chaos and confusion, exacerbated by weeks of hard riding and the stress of imminent combat, troopers and officers may have confused Kanipe's words with Martin. Regardless of Martin's exact words to Benteen's orderly or Company H troopers, the message he carried was the second plea for Benteen to advance with speed to Custer.

PART III

THE FINAL YEARS

Chapter Ten

The Hilltop

After he received Cooke's note and briefly questioned Martin, Benteen passed it to three other officers who had come up from their companies. Each one scanned the dispatch but offered no reply before passing it on; the last officer handed it back to Benteen who pocketed the message.[1]

Benteen and his three companies began moving in the general direction of the village, but upon reaching a high ridge, they watched "... an immense number of Indians on the plain, mounted of course and charging down on some dismounted men of Major Reno's command." Reno's battalion had attacked one end of the village, but their assault was quickly repulsed and they were "flying for dear life." As they retreated across the Little Bighorn and clambered up the steep bluffs to a position now called Reno Hill, Benteen led his men to their relief and "... a more delighted lot of folks you never saw."[2]

"For God's sake, Benteen, halt your command and wait until I can organize my men," exclaimed Reno. Benteen pulled Cooke's dispatch from his pocket and showed it to Reno, his superior officer. The Major, "bareheaded and much excited" after his wild retreat, replied, "Well I have lost about half of my men, and I could do no better than I have done."[3] In their disorder confusion, unable to form a skirmish line, the shattered remnants of Reno's command was saved by the timely arrival of Benteen.

The combined battalions of Reno and Benteen paused on the hill as they waited for the pack train. Gunfire from the direction of Custer's position increased, and many troopers claimed they heard two volleys of rifle fire. Some believed Custer was "giving it to them." Before the pack train arrived, a sortie to find Custer - it was initiated by Captain Weir but eventually joined by the entire command - made its way to a small hill two miles to the north. The rise (Weir Point) allowed the troopers to see most of the valley to the north where Custer's men were thought to be fighting, but swirling dust and smoke from rifle fire obscured much of their view. When a large group of mounted warriors was spotted heading in their direction, the combined command retreated to their original position further south, but not without some difficulty for Martin. "His horse was spouting blood from a bullet wound in his right hip but Martini didn't know anything about it," wrote Private Charles Windolph, "[Martin's] horse was played out and it was all that he could do to keep up with us."[4]

"We withdrew to a saucer like hill, putting our horses and packs in the bottom of saucer and threw all of our force dismounted around this corral," Benteen explained to his wife.[5] The elevated position was mostly barren with "no trees, rocks, mounds, or such, just an occasional scraggly sagebrush or prickly pear cactus, along with knee high grass that was quickly trampled flat."[6] Benteen's men divided their ammunition with Reno's, who had expended most of theirs. The ammunition and other supplies from the pack mules arrived an hour later. Nearly 350 troopers, including Martin, eventually reached the hilltop.

A view of the Little Bighorn River and valley from Reno Hill. After Martin delivered Cooke's message, he remained here with Reno and Benteen's combined columns where they successfully fought off attacks and enfilading fire for two days until relieved by General Terry's column. (*Courtesy of Dan J. Davis*)

Reno's men guarded the north rim while Benteen secured the south with the still-intact Company H. McDougall (Company B) and Captain Thomas French's Company M were posted on the western edge of the position, while Captain Myles Moylan and Company A defended the east perimeter. The soldiers hurriedly strengthened their position, but the task of digging rifle pits proved difficult since there were "only three or four spades and shovels in the whole command."[7] As the warriors closed in, cursing and sweating soldiers frantically scraped the hard ground with anything at hand to create cover from the enemy fire; many men improvised breastworks from saddles, boxes of hardtack, sacks of bacon, and bags of forage.[8] Wounded horses and mules were shot by desperate troopers and dragged into position to provide more cover.

Darkness finally fell between 9:00 and 10:00 p.m. and the gunfire slackened. Twelve troopers had been killed on the hilltop with another twenty wounded.[9] As they continued to fortify their position, the sounds emanating from the valley unnerved many troopers. "Their camp was a veritable pandemonium," Lieutenant Godfrey recalled, "All night long they continued their frantic revels: beating tom-toms, dancing, whooping, yelling with demoniacal screams, and discharging firearms." The men had little rest that night, their fears inflamed by the celebration below. Godfrey gravely added, "We knew they were having a scalp dance."[10]

At midnight, Martin was ordered by Reno to sound Reveille at 2:00 a.m. (June 26). The Indians initially replied with a weak fusillade, but as the sun rose, their fire increased. The hours passed slowly for the besieged troopers. Sweating heavily in the unrelenting heat, the swirling dust choked and caked them; and, silhouetted against the sun, the troopers seemed like ashen ghosts. By 11:00 a.m., Lieutenant Godfrey remarked, "The excitement and heat made our thirst almost maddening ... They put pebbles in their mouths to excite the glands; some ate grass roots, but did not find relief. Some tried to eat hard bread, but after chewing it awhile would blow it out of their mouths like so much flour. A few potatoes were given out and afforded some relief."[11] In an effort to relieve their agony, especially for the wounded, troopers volunteered to retrieve water from the river beneath their position. At noon, as the water parties dashed down to the river, sharpshooters from Martin's Company provided covering fire. For their valor, twenty-four men were awarded the Medal of Honor.

Benteen was not among the recipients despite his determined and courageous leadership during the hilltop fight. As Reno mostly cowered in the center of the position, Benteen repeatedly exposed himself to enemy fire. At one point, Martin told Camp that after

Benteen's boot heel was shot off, the Captain coolly replied, "Pretty close call -- try again."[12] Throughout the day, warriors crept closer - hidden in the tall grass and gullies - massing to attack; a few drew close enough to throw clods of dirt and rocks at the troopers. To disperse the Indians before they stormed the position, Benteen led two different charges down the hill. "We charged out," Martin remembered, "old Benteen right in front of us."[13] After the battle, most troopers credited Benteen for saving the command.

Another photograph of the Little Bighorn River taken from the Seventh Cavalry's defensive position on Reno Hill. Bayonet charges and suicide missions to obtain water for the wounded and dying were the norm. (*Courtesy of Dan J. Davis*)

By 1:00 p.m., Godfrey recalled, "The Indians had nearly all left us, but they still guarded the river."[14] The warriors returned within the hour and resumed their attack, but by 3:00 p.m., the shooting stopped entirely. A few hours later, anxious troopers watched as an "immense cavalcade of people and horses began to move leisurely from the village up the valley," and away from their position.[15] Some soldiers estimated that the massive movement included thousands of Indians and an enormous pony herd.

"The stench from the dead men and horses was now exceedingly offensive," Godfrey remarked, "and it was decided to take up a new position nearer the river." He calculated the command's losses to be 18 troopers killed with another fifty-two wounded.[16] Martin's Company H suffered the most on that first day; their exposed position the subject of long-range fire from nearby hills. Martin testified at the

1879 Inquiry that during the second day of the siege, he was "the only one that sounded the calls." The Seventh's trumpeters paid an especially heavy toll: Eleven were killed during the two-day battle, including Custer's Chief Trumpeter Henry Voss. The other trumpeter from Company H, William Ramell, was badly wounded during the hilltop siege.

"After the Indians left that evening," Martin stated, "I sounded retreat, recall and march, as there might be some of our friends in the ravines."[17] Still they wondered about Custer's whereabouts. Many believed he had escaped but would return with one of the other columns. They would learn in a few hours that Custer and over 210 Seventh Cavalry troopers, civilians and scouts lay dead on the gentle hills by the Little Bighorn River.

CHAPTER ELEVEN

The Fate of Custer

In the early morning of June 27, the men were able to eat in relative quiet, but when a large dust cloud was observed at 9:30 a.m., they feared the warriors had returned. Martin was ordered to sound his bugle, and the command's apprehension turned to relief when the proper reply call was heard. A solitary scout approached their position and confirmed that General Terry and a relief column had arrived. Martin's diary added it was "too late for Custer and just in time for us - for we were about 400 against 5,000."[1]

As General Terry's column neared their position, "... their coming was greeted with prolonged hearty cheers," wrote Godfrey, but their joyous mood quickly changed, "The grave countenance of the General [Terry] awed the men to silence."[2] Terry's column had found the bodies of Custer and his command on their way to Reno Hill. Many troopers wept at the news, while others refused to believe the reports. It seemed impossible that Custer had not escaped, but had instead been trapped and killed.

Later that morning, Reno introduced Martin to General Terry, "This is the man who carried the last dispatch, General." Terry queried Martin for several minutes on Custer's last position and movements. Satisfied with the bugler's responses, Terry thanked him and added, "Well, you are a lucky man and I wish you good fortune."[3] Martin probably served with Reno's headquarters staff after reaching the hilltop, necessitated by the loss of eleven buglers killed with at least one more wounded. His proximity to Reno as orderly - within two yards of the Major at all times - created an opportunity for Reno to introduce Martin to General Terry.

In the early afternoon, many of the men who survived the hilltop siege rode to what became known as Last Stand Hill. "When we got to the place where they had made their stand," Martin wrote of H Company's first view of the battleground, "we found everything dead except Captain Keogh's horse." The brutality and violence of the fight was evident by the frightful carnage, he recalled, "The men had been cut and mangled badly, heads all smashed in, arms and legs twisted like rope, and twenty or thirty arrows struck in each body." The hot sun had bloated most of corpses, and Martin remembered, "It was the worst sight imaginable." The extensive mutilations made it difficult for them to identify their fallen comrades among the dead; some men were identified by a tattoo or bit of clothing. Martin recorded when they found the body of Custer, "Toward the middle of the battleground, we found the body of Custer's grey horse, with the general's head resting on its stomach." General Custer was dead, Martin wrote, killed by "a bullet hole in his left breast and one other in his right temple."[4]

News of the battle - 'Custer's Last Stand' as it would be known - spread from Fort Lincoln to Chicago to New York. As the initial shock faded, cries for revenge followed with the public's fury fueled by the press. "It is time to quit this Sunday-school policy … and exterminate every Indian who will not remain upon the reservations," declared the *Chicago Daily Tribune* in an article published one week after the battle, "The best use to make of an Indian who will not stay on a reservation is to kill him." Even Custer's reputation was sullied as the same *Chicago Daily Tribune* columnist asserted, "The Indian will never by subdued by such madcap charges as that made by Custer."[5] Retribution was the order of the day and over the next few years, troops streamed into the Black Hills and surrounding regions. Recalcitrant native warriors and their families were corralled into government reservations; any who resisted were hunted down and killed without hesitation.

Following the battle, Martin and other Seventh Regiment survivors remained in the Dakota Territory, encamped by the Yellowstone River while new officers and recruits refilled their ranks. In early August, the Seventh decamped and spent several futile weeks searching for hostile tribes before turning back for their base. The demoralized Regiment straggled into Fort Lincoln on September 26. Martin continued to serve as trumpeter of Company H – still under the command of Benteen – over the next three years. Reinforcements continued to arrive and by 1877, the newly reconstituted Seventh Cavalry Regiment campaigned successfully against Chief Joseph and the Nez Percé with key victories at the battles of Bear Paw and Canyon Creek.

CHAPTER TWELVE

The Court of Inquiry

The Battle of the Little Bighorn did not end in 1876. It would be fought again and again over the years with newspapers and books replacing bullets and arrows. On January 13, 1879, the battle resumed at a Court of Inquiry, convened by the U.S. Army to investigate the conduct of Major Marcus Reno during the two-day conflict. Reno demanded the public forum to defend his actions, which included allegations of drunkenness. Many of the surviving officers and enlisted men, including Martin, traveled to the Palmer House, a Chicago hotel, to offer their testimony at the Inquiry, which ran from January 13 through February 11, 1879.

On a frigid Friday afternoon, Martin testified at the Court of Inquiry, the last of several witnesses to appear on January 31. He was asked approximately 150 questions, although many were the same question restated differently.[1] Elements of Martin's testimony lacked consistency, prompting doubts of his truthfulness. The imperfect quality of his English may have played a role, and perhaps not all of "... his heavily accented replies were rendered with accuracy for the record."[2] Transcription of the Inquiry's proceedings was poorly handled, and the Army did not officially record the Inquiry. Instead, several reporters jotted testimony into their notebooks and filled in the blanks afterwards. According to Martin, Benteen erred when he testified that the bugler was ordered back to 'hurry up' the pack train after delivering his dispatch. "I told them so at Chicago in 1879 when they had the Court of Inquiry," he explained to Colonel Graham, "but I didn't speak English so good then, and they misunderstood me and made the report of my testimony show that I took an order to [the pack train]. But that is a mistake."[3]

Language issues aside, Martin's less than perfect recollections "... ought to have been better, but since he was treated like an idiot at that forum, there is little guarantee that he was questioned with clarity."[4] It is difficult to discern emotions from the transcripts alone, but the following exchange appeared to serve little purpose other than trivializing Martin's testimony:

The Court: Did not time seem long to you then?
Martin: Yes, sir, sometimes.
The Court: Does not time seem longer when you are not doing anything than when you are?
Martin: Sometimes it goes fast and sometimes it goes slow.

In 1908, during his first interview with Camp, Martin claimed he did not include the encounter with Boston Custer during the Court of Inquiry testimony "because he was not asked the question." Camp concluded that, in Martin's opinion, "... it was not desired that he should tell all he knew."[5] Martin offered no further clarification on the subject, but his comments of the Court of Inquiry and its aftermath suggest he felt slighted by the inattention.

Adhering to their code of honor, the officers closed ranks and what actually occurred at the Little Bighorn remained hidden behind by testimonies riddled with half-truths. The Court's motivation in finding the truth played a large role during the proceedings, but "... the truth was very hard to come by."[6] Benteen's testimony was "chock-full of holes, untruths and contradictions," yet the Court failed to pursue his often conflicting testimony.[7] Martin's own replies on the amount of time it took to deliver Cooke's message varied widely (between 15 minutes and one hour), but the Court again failed to seek clarification. Many have speculated that Martin and others were 'coached' on their testimony. One of the officers of the court summarized the proceedings: "The officers wouldn't tell us anything, and we could nothing more than damn Reno with faint praise."[8] In early March 1879, the Court of Inquiry published its findings and Reno was absolved of any wrongdoing. Over the course of a long interview in 1906, Martin showed the reporter a copy of a report from the proceedings. "Martin's name is that of the only witness mentioned," offered the reporter, "it was his testimony that swung the balance into Reno's favor."[9]

Despite Martin's perceived failings, as noted by Benteen, the bugler remained in the Captain's Company H until his scheduled discharge on May 31, 1879. As Benteen's trumpeter, he would have been in close proximity to the Captain on a daily basis. Were Martin incapable of performing his duties, the ever-critical Benteen would have transferred him to another company or regiment if for no other reason than the Captain's own safety and that of his command.

CHAPTER THIRTEEN

Fort McHenry

The year of 1879 was rather significant for John Martin. After he testified at the Court of Inquiry, Martin rejoined the Seventh Regiment at Fort Lincoln for a few months until he was honorably discharged on May 31, 1879, after completing his original five-year enlistment. "When we were mustered out," he recalled, "we all turned in our equipment and I gave up everything except the bugle which was my own personal property." He was also presented with a written recommendation from Captain Benteen; the parchment document contained a "long list of the engagements he took part in ... the word 'excellent' underscored after his character qualification."[1]

Three weeks later, Martin re-enlisted for another five years as a trumpeter with the Third Artillery Regiment, Battery G, stationed at Fort Schulyer in the Bronx, one of the five boroughs of New York City. He never explained his decision not to re-enlist with the Seventh. Perhaps, the memories of the Little Bighorn weighed on him; or, he may have tired of the hard life of a cavalry trooper. A more plausible explanation may have been his relationship with Julia Margaret Higgins, a 19-year-old Irish girl from Oswego, New York. They met while he served at Fort Schuyler.

Following a short engagement, John and Julia were married at St. Raymond's Catholic Church in Westchester County (New York) on October 7 by a Reverend McEvoy; the ceremony was witnessed by Lorenzo and Dillory Thomassi. In 1880, while stationed on coastal defense duty in St. Augustine, Florida, the Martins welcomed their first child, Julia. A son followed three years later, and Martin's diary revealed the boy was named George in honor of the fallen Seventh Cavalry commander.

In late June 1884, Martin re-enlisted for another five years with the Third Artillery Regiment. The Martins remained in St. Augustine until the regiment was transferred to Fort McHenry in Baltimore, Maryland. Initially they lived in the tight confines of the Fort's quarters, but soon settled into their own home at 1410 Woodall Street, not far from the Fort, in the Locust Point section of south Baltimore. Martin's role at the Little Bighorn boosted his status within the community. To the public, John Martin performed his duty and his reputation remained unsullied by the Army's Court of Inquiry. A Baltimore newspaper article reported on the physical appearance of Fort McHenry proudly added that Martin - "Sole Survivor of the Custer Massacre" - was now stationed there.[2]

Perhaps bored by the tedium of peacetime service in a heavy artillery battery, Martin traveled to Washington, D.C., in October 1886. He hoped to obtain a messenger position with the War Department. "A neatly dressed artilleryman named Martin, the sole white survivor of Custer's command," noted a *New York Times* reporter, paid a visit to General Philip Sheridan's office at the War Department. Sheridan, Commanding General of the U.S. Army, "promised to further his [Martin's] application as far as it lay in his power to do so."[3] Since Martin remained with his artillery unit at Fort McHenry, Sheridan's assistance was unsuccessful.

Martin continued his service with the Third Artillery Regiment, but transferred to a different unit (Battery D) on December 22, 1892. He returned to Washington with the Third Artillery for the parade celebrating the inauguration of President Grover Cleveland on March 4, 1893. A journalist assigned to report on the parade observed, "On the extreme left of the front rank ... marched a bronzed and rugged featured veteran who would have received a share of plaudits on his own account had his history been known. His name was John Martin and he was the only survivor of the Custer massacre."[4]

He transferred into Battery L of the Fourth Artillery on April 14, 1893, followed by another move to Battery D of the Fourth Artillery in November of that year. Martin's transfers may have been driven by a desire to remain stationed at Fort McHenry, a result of a rapidly growing family that required his patriarchal attention. He re-enlisted for a three-year commitment with Battery D of the Fourth Artillery in late June 1894, and again in 1897; enlistment commitments had been reduced from five years to three. In 1898, at the outbreak of the Spanish-American War, Martin's Artillery Regiment was transferred to Tampa, Florida, before being sent on to Cuba.

In 1906, a reporter from the *New York Evening Post* met with Martin at his Brooklyn apartment. During their long interview, the reporter spotted a "battered and slightly tarnished" saber hanging on the wall and asked Martin to explain its significance. "I was in Cuba during the Spanish war," he replied, "when my sergeant called me into his tent and said, 'John, you were with Custer. I have a relic from his command and I am going to give it to you.' Then he brought out this saber and I took and looked at it carefully." Martin examined every part of the saber - issued to all cavalrymen - for some identification. Under the bell guard, by the hilt, "I found my initials, J.D.M., with the date 'June, 1876' where I had scratched them with a nail years ago." The saber's return delighted Martin, "I was mighty glad to get it back," he told the reporter.[5] The saber story appears dubious for several reasons: Who was Martin's Sergeant and why would he bring the saber to Cuba almost 24 years after the Battle of the Little Bighorn? No further details of the saber were included, but the reporter may have been distracted by another memento from the Spanish-American War in Martin's apartment. A cornet that hung on a wall, Martin explained, once belonged to a Spanish bugler who gave it to Martin after the truce because [Martin] "could play it better than its owner."[6]

By 1900, the Martins had moved to 1321 Hull Street, a row house close to Fort McHenry.[7] Their move may have been necessitated by an expanding family; after the births of Julia and George, the family welcomed Mary (or Mollie as she was called), Jane, May, John Jr., Frank and Lawrence. John remained in Cuba with the Fourth Artillery Regiment until September 30, 1900, when he re-enlisted with the rank of Corporal in a familiar unit, Company H of the Seventh Regiment. Maybe Martin encountered former comrades from the Seventh in Cuba, who encouraged him to rejoin the unit. At nearly fifty years in age, he was too old for active campaigning and saddled with familial responsibilities; his enlistment, therefore, appears more honorific than practical. Although Company H remained in Cuba until May 1902, Martin did not, and on June 15, 1901, he transferred to Company 39 of the recently created Coastal Artillery Corps, culled from existing units including Martin's Fourth Artillery Regiment. One month later, he moved to Company 90 (also Coastal Artillery Corps), stationed at Fort McHenry, and returned to Baltimore.

Corporal John Martin received a final promotion - to Master Sergeant - prior to his mandatory retirement (due to age limitation) on January 7, 1904. After thirty years of continuous military service, he left the Army and prepared for the next phase of his life. His retirement drew the attention of the press, and several newspapers noted Martin's pension of "three quarters of his regular pay [roughly $30 per month]." When he left the service, Martin carried a "bundle of recommendations ... from the various captains and other officers under whom he has served." The documents were consistent, a reporter asserted, in their high appraisal of Martin's character.[8]

CHAPTER FOURTEEN

Baltimore and Brooklyn

Following his retirement from the Army, John and Julia opened a small confectionery shop on Fort Avenue, near the gates of Fort McHenry.[1] Although the three eldest children had moved out, five continued to live in the Martin home on Hull Street: Jane, May, John Jr., Frank and Lawrence. With many mouths still to feed, the Martins hoped the shop would supplement his Army pension. After three decades of military service, Martin tried to adjust to his new life as husband, father and shopkeeper. Despite his best efforts, however, Martin failed in his new role.

During the first few years of artillery service, Martin's duties required him to remain at the base or Fort and his time away from home was limited. By the latter years of his service, especially with the onset of Spanish-American War, he was absent for extended periods. While he was away, many of the decisions affecting the family were left to Julia. Upon his return, he may have felt his authority as family patriarch devalued by Julia's control over the household.

Alternately, John Martin's first years as a foundling affected him, perhaps even rendering him emotionally incapable of guiding his family. The pressing needs of his children, possibly even the demands of Julia, may have been too much for John to handle. The role he assumed - a family man, with all its attendant duties and responsibilities - simply may not have suited Martin, whose admittedly undefined youth and family relationship may have had some bearing. Nevertheless, John Martin's life transformed once more and he returned - alone - to his first American home, Brooklyn. Determining when he left Baltimore is difficult. Martin was still in Baltimore when he left the Army in 1904, but had arrived in New York by mid-June 1906. A journalist from the *Brooklyn Standard Union* noted in late June 1906 that Martin had been living in the borough for a few years.[2]

The allure of New York played a part in his decision to leave Baltimore. Martin's acclaim as the 'sole survivor of the Custer massacre' was enhanced and glamorized in New York, less so in Baltimore. A myriad of new opportunities greeted John Martin when he returned to New York in 1906, unlike his first arrival when the country was enduring the ordeal of the Panic of 1873. A contemporary reporter surmised Martin returned to New York because "he missed hearing the Italian spoken back in Brooklyn."[3] While Baltimore boasted a sizeable Italian population, many more Italians made Brooklyn their home and perhaps Martin missed hearing the Campania dialect of his youth.

Initially, Martin moved into an apartment or rented room at 58 York Street in the Vinegar Hill section of Brooklyn. Originally, an Irish enclave, the Vinegar Hill neighborhood had begun to transform by 1906 as a new wave of Italian immigrants settled in.[4] A reporter who visited Martin's Brooklyn residence in 1906 described his room as "modestly furnished - many people would say poorly." On Martin's walls hung reminders of his life in the cavalry including the Regimental saber, the Spanish bugler's cornet, and an 1874 photograph of General Custer "yellow and grimy with age and exposure."[5] Another prized possession also had a home on the wall: The cavalry bugle issued to him 32 years earlier when a young John Martin first reported for duty at Jefferson Barracks. "He has not forgotten how to sound martial strains upon his bugle," the reporter noted that while Martin still practiced many of the cavalry calls, his favorite remained 'Taps.'[6]

After he settled in Brooklyn, Martin looked for work. One newspaper account claimed he had been "filling a clerical position for a livelihood."[7] By July 1906, however, Martin began a new job as a ticket agent for the New York City subway; the new transportation system was operated by the Interborough Rapid Transit Company. He obtained the position with the help of Major Francis M. Gibson of the New York Street Cleaning Department. Gibson had served as First Lieutenant in Benteen's Company H and knew Martin well. The ticket agent position, however, was not Martin's first choice for employment.

"About a week ago I got a card from the navy yard saying they had heard I was a retired veteran, and offering me a job," Martin told a reporter in September 1906. He quit the subway job and went to the Brooklyn Navy Yard. "The man in charge told me the job ... was to shovel coal while the warships were getting their supplies," he explained, but the job would only last ten days and "they wouldn't need me anymore." Martin was taken aback by the offer. "Of course

I am strong enough, but I never shoveled coal in my life," he said, "It was a funny way for the Government to try to reward me." Martin proudly added, "I did not ask for help in the first place, so I turned around and walked out." He was allowed to return as his job on the subway as Gateman 02141.[8]

John Martin arose early each morning and dutifully donned his subway agent uniform. He walked to the closest station at the time, near the Brooklyn Bridge, and rode to the 103rd Street Station in upper Manhattan. As a ticket agent, he worked a twelve-hour daily shift, and while "… has a good living [was] assured," it was exceedingly "monotonous work from 7 o'clock in the morning until 7 [o'clock] in the evening."[9] The job paid him $45 per month, and when combined with his Army pension, John Martin pocketed $75 every month.

As riders entered the station, they deposited their tickets into a glass-topped receptacle as Martin - a 'ticket chopper' as subway agents were called - raised and lowered a lever that chopped or shredded the tickets.[10] Many of the riders knew him personally and were greeted with "a regulation military salute" from Martin, described as "still an active clear-eyed man whose strong face and perfect poise clearly indicate the active and perfect training he has had since infancy … he is straight and sturdy as ever."[11] Often, the reporter added, passengers lingered "for a minute with the old veteran of at least three active campaigns." He earned friends among the Interborough Rapid Transit officials who tried to ease some of his misery and a small booth was "erected to protect him from the wintry drafts which sweep through the opening to the street."[12]

A strong attraction to New York, and what it could offer him, impacted Martin's decision to remain. He was a favorite of reporters who interviewed and reported regularly on his activities; editors almost universally used the same title or byline for stories on Martin: "Sole Survivor of the Custer Massacre." From their accounts, a portrait of John Martin emerged. "A trifle under medium height, with clear, brown eyes, iron grey hair and a short-cropped moustache," one journalist observed, "[Martin] does not look his 53 years by half a score."[13] A correspondent from the *Brooklyn Standard Union* opined, "Martin has weathered well all the storms of life … He does not look the years that have passed him by and is bright and cheerful." The article closed dramatically, "He is a product of war, and saw the grim god at his worst."[14]

On many nights, after his long shift at the subway station had ended, John Martin rode the train to Broadway. As his celebrity expanded, Martin added to his income with appearances on Broadway stages, often at the request of stage managers and producers. To the delight of theatregoers, Martin played various bugle calls or regaled the patrons with stories of his time with Custer, the Seventh Cavalry and the Little Bighorn between acts or during intermission. His time on Broadway was not limited to appearing on the stage, and reporters noted many events in which Martin was an honored guest. In February 1907, Martin was feted with "his old regiment, the Seventh Cavalry, and other military organizations in full uniform attended a 'military night' of a popular play a few nights ago ..."[15] Later that year, a newspaper reported that the American Theatre honored Martin during their production of "Custer's Last Fight."[16] The attention must have been intoxicating, especially to a man who began life as a forgotten *trovatello* destined for a life in poverty.

When not on Broadway or at work, Martin participated in functions and events sponsored by one of several veterans' organizations of which he was a member. He traveled with fellow Seventh Regiment veterans each year to West Point on the anniversary of the Little Bighorn where, "... the famous bugle which sang 'Boots and Saddles' so cheerily over many a forgotten camping ground ... played 'Taps' over Custer's grave."[17] The Charles F. Roe Garrison of the Army and Navy Union, in particular, hosted many events where Martin displayed his bugling skills. On August 20, 1907, Martin attended a Seventh Cavalry reunion in Canandaigua, New York. The *Geneva Daily Times* reported on the elaborate festivities scheduled for the two-day event. Mrs. Elizabeth Custer accepted an invitation, the article noted, and 'Bugler' John Martin – "the last white man to see Custer alive" – would play his bugle at the ceremonies.[18]

Despite several interviews during this period, Martin remained quiet on the subject of his wife and family in Baltimore. His reticence may have hidden a darker secret: In 1908, a scandalous rumor surfaced, set in motion by an article published in the *Brooklyn Eagle*.[19] The allegation claimed Martin had an affair with a Baltimore woman of "loose" morals, and may have contracted venereal disease from her as a result.[20] When Julia discovered the affair, Martin was forced to leave their Baltimore home and found his way to New York.

Julia Martin, the journalist reported, later contacted and implored the police to help her locate John Martin; she hoped he "might be induced to help her in the matter" of their three small children. "She told the police that the last she heard from him," the account continued, Martin was working in the subway. A Sergeant Thurston, presumably an officer with the Brooklyn police, traced Martin to a "furnished room" at 168 Prospect Street. During his questioning, Martin said there was no ill will against his wife, and the reporter noted he "seemed to be really pleased that she was alive and well." Martin left Baltimore because "[Julia] had driven him away ... and told him that she did not want to hear from him anymore." Martin felt this relieved him of his marital duties, and while he "would be glad to tender help" to their children, he declared that as far as Julia was concerned, "He was not going back to her and that was the end of it." After he notified Julia Martin of John's Brooklyn address, the article concluded, Sergeant Thurston declared the matter closed.[21]

While certain aspects of the story have merit, a spate of misleading 'facts' as represented in the *Brooklyn Daily Eagle* article raises suspicion of the journalist's reliability and professionalism.[22] The piece confirmed that Martin had moved to a rented room located at 168 Prospect Street (where he would remain until his death fifteen years later). Lacking any further evidence, what really occurred remains a matter of conjecture and speculation. Martin's granddaughters believed he moved to Brooklyn because he had "a married daughter Mary (Mollie) living there and was able to find work more easily." His wife, Julia, did not like New York and chose to remain in Baltimore, but traveled "back and forth to Brooklyn, staying with daughter Mollie."[23] Their eldest daughter, Julia, who was employed by a railroad company in New York, provided free rail passes. He was a "very nice man," one granddaughter fondly remembered and liked to play an accordion when they visited. By all indications, John Martin's children remained close to him, and he returned their affections. Lacking any further evidence other than their recollections, what really occurred remains a matter of conjecture and speculation.[24]

Whether through his own initiative or with the assistance of another, Martin's second trip to the Brooklyn Navy Yard in 1911 proved more successful than his first visit in 1906. His fame as Custer's last messenger was "brought to the attention of the authorities [in] Washington," a reporter declared, "and a position was found for him." He readily traded his subway job for a less taxing one as a mechanic's assistant at the Yard. The new position eliminated the long daily commute to the 103rd Street Station in Manhattan; another benefit to an aging Martin was the Navy Yard's proximity to his home (less than a mile). Martin's acclaim as Custer's bugler drew the interest of his co-workers: In April 1914, members of the George Bleck Association, a fraternal organization for Navy Yard employees, attended a lecture by fellow member John Martin. His bona fides were confirmed at the conclusion of the lecture, a reporter noted, when Martin "produced convincing documentary evidence tending to substantiate his claims."[25]

John Martin (Giovanni Martino) in an undated photo-graph. Based on his appearance, the photograph was likely taken shortly before Martin's death in 1922.
(*Courtesy of Claudio Busi and Patricia Gordon Ditch*)

He remained a favorite of parade organizers and schoolchildren well into his late 60s. Sergeant John Martin, "a grizzled old man," observed one reporter during the Liberty Loan parade in New York City in April 1918, "… reclined in an automobile float filled with children."[26] As Martin grew older and less mobile, Brooklyn schoolchildren were brought to his apartment to hear of his exploits at the

Battle of the Little Bighorn. When his general health declined in 1918, Martin was forced to curtail his active participation with many groups; and, he likely gave up his Navy Yard job at this time. A newspaper reported that Martin, the bugler for the Brooklyn Camp garrison of the Spanish War Veterans, was too ill to attend a memorial service in mid-May 1918.[27]

In 1920, the sixty-eight year old Martin lived with the Cicco family at 168 Prospect Street. Census records listed him as an "uncle-in-law" of the Cicco family. Although he remained estranged from his wife, Julia, the records continued to list Martin as married.[28] The Cicco family consisted of Joseph, his wife Clara, and their seven children; aside from renting a room in their home, Martin's connection to the family is unknown and he does not appear to have been directly related. Pasquale Petrocelli considered the "uncle-in-law" designation insignificant and a relic of the patriarchal system; it was an honorary title meant to show deference to the true head of the household, Joseph Cicco. The Prospect Street address was referenced in the 1908 *Brooklyn Eagle* article that reported on the efforts of Brooklyn detectives who tracked him down at Julia's request.[29] This would indicate Martin had lived at the same address in Brooklyn for nearly fifteen years.

As for John Martin's own family, May and Lawrence (and likely John, Jr.) remained in Baltimore close to their mother. Daughters Julia and Mary (Mollie) were both married and lived in Brooklyn, not far from their father's apartment; they may have even preceded John's arrival in 1905 or 1906. John and Julia's first son, George, an Army officer and was stationed at Fort Adams, Rhode Island; he retired after attaining the rank of General. Another son, Frank, was an officer in the Marine Corps and assigned to Fort Howard, Maryland.

CHAPTER FIFTEEN

Taps

In his life, Martin had escaped the poverty of southern Italy and survived the massacre at the Little Bighorn, but the streets of Brooklyn, combined with his advanced age and failing health, proved too much to overcome. On December 18, 1922, John Martin was struck by a truck (or taxi) as he crossed a street near his Brooklyn home. He was hospitalized at the Cumberland Street Hospital, located by the Brooklyn-Queens Expressway in Brooklyn. While the injuries he sustained were severe, a more devastating medical issue was discovered and for six days John Martin struggled for his life from complications arising from a serious bronchial pulmonary condition. His fight ended at 10:15 on Sunday morning, December 24, 1922. Only a son-in-law (Mary's husband) was present when John Martin - Giovanni Martino - passed away at the age of 69. Martin was survived by his widow, four daughters, four sons, and several grandchildren. The funeral was held at the home of his eldest daughter, Julia Martin Jensen, at 2:00 p.m. on the following day.[1]

Trooper John Martin's last ride ended at Cypress Hills National Cemetery in Brooklyn on December 27, 1922, where he was buried with full military honors in the veterans section.[2] His family was joined at the funeral by Martin's fellow Seventh Cavalry troopers, as well as veterans from assorted Army and Navy Union groups, including the Charles F. Roe and General George A. Custer Garrisons. The Army placed a granite headstone at his grave that bore the understated inscription:

John Martin
Italy
Sgt [Sergeant]
90 Coast Artillery
December 24, 1922

In a final irony, John Martin may have died on the very same date of his actual birth: December 24. It remains a question that will never be answered.

In 1991, the borough of Brooklyn hosted a memorial service at Martin's gravesite. The keynote speech was delivered by Donald Horn of the Little Big Horn Associates, one of several organizations dedicated to the study and research of the battle and its participants. Horn considered the original standard military headstone too modest, and received permission to replace it. Before engraving the new, more ornate headstone, Horn asked the late Ron Hartman, John Martin's great grandson, which name to use.[3] His grandfather, Hartman replied, was "proud of his adopted country" and would have wanted his American name, John Martin, imprinted. On a sunny mid-summer day in 1991, the new headstone was unveiled at Cypress Hills in a ceremony attended by many of Martin's relatives, several members of the Little Big Horn Associates and local elected officials; a Catholic priest blessed the event while the Brooklyn American Legion provided an honor and color guard. In light of Martin's legacy, Horn commented, "It was a fitting tribute."[4]

The original headstone was laid in front of the new headstone, and serves as a footstone. Martin's new headstone bears the following inscription:

John Martin
Sgt. U.S. 7th Cavalry
Died Dec. 24, 1922

Carried Gen. Custer's
Last Message
Battle of Little Big Horn
June 25, 1876

Shortly after his death, Martin's widow, Julia, applied for an Army pension assignment. In order to validate her claim as his wife, Julia was required to provide proof that their separation was only that, and not a divorce. Depositions were collected from family and neighbors by the Army Pension Board, and the Rector of St. Raymond's, Edward McKenna, issued a replacement Certificate of Marriage as validation. The matter was resolved in Julia's favor on March 23, 1923. Unfortunately, Julia began to suffer from dementia and was declared insane in September 1924; she spent her remaining years confined to the Spring Grove Hospital in Catonsville, Maryland.

The original headstone (left) at John Martin's grave in the veterans section at the Cypress Hills National Cemetery in Brooklyn, New York. The stone was replaced by Don Horn and the Little Big Horn Associates with the more detailed larger headstone in 1991 (bottom right).

(*Courtesy of Charles E. Merkel, Jr.*)

Detail of new headstone's inscription.
(*Courtesy of W. Donald Horn*)

Critical assessments of Martin tend to portray him as an ignorant immigrant who tried to hide his poor English skills through contradictory statements. With few defenders, the Italian-born Martin became a convenient target, some of which originated from bigoted and racist attitudes consistent with the era. The acerbic Captain Benteen once described Martin as a "thick headed, dull witted Italian, just as much cut out for a cavalryman as he was for a king."[5] The trumpeter's admiration of Custer certainly placed him in the crosshairs of Benteen and his denigrating remarks. Martin, however, was unjustly "… criticized for failing to move the immovable [Benteen]."[6] Much of the criticism is inaccurate and poorly reasoned, and places an overreliance on the shaky Court of Inquiry's transcripts or minor misstatements.

However, questions regarding Martin's varying renditions of the events have merit. Was he inscrutable by design or default? As the years passed, Martin happily continued to be interviewed by historians, researchers and journalists regarding his memories of the Little Bighorn. Perhaps thoughtlessly, he occasionally amended a few details of the battle and his life; yet, his intent was often an honest effort to correct an inaccuracy or discrepancy in the deposition taken at the 1879 Court of Inquiry. Language issues complicated his ability to express properly what he saw and heard, more so earlier in his life than his later years. Nevertheless, Martin's memory was "sharper and truer than that of many men who would pass themselves off" as superior to him.[7] Ultimately, John Martin remained consistent in his narration, despite some obvious yet minor embellishments.

Colonel Graham recalled that Martin was "… very old and very feeble when I found him deep in the jungle of Brooklyn's Italian quarter [in 1922]," and his memory, "as feeble as his body." Graham visited Martin three times, "each time reading to him (for he was almost blind) his testimony before the Reno Inquiry." Although Martin's memory wavered initially, Graham concluded, "… when it did come back, it came with a wealth of incident and detail that was surprising. And so I wrote his story, just as he told it to me."[8] Martin's narrative from the Graham interviews is quite detailed, and not significantly different from his 1908 and 1910 interviews with Walter Mason Camp.

Through the collaborative and solo efforts of many, John Martin - Giovanni Martino - has not been forgotten and interest in his life continues, especially in his native Italy. Italians hold great admiration and pride for Martin, *il trombettiere di Custer,* as evidenced by their research and eagerness to make his story known. The most important discoveries resulted from the diligent efforts of Italian researchers, historians and journalists: Professor Giuseppe Colitti, Dr. Michele Esposito, Pasquale Petrocelli, and Claudio Busi.

Admiration for Martin extends to his adopted land, as well. On May 28, 1999, Martin's service was recognized and honored by the Arlington National Cemetery's Taps Project, a permanent exhibit created by Air Force Master Sergeant and Trumpeter Jari A. Villanueva (retired) which pays tribute to nine famous buglers in U.S.

Army history.[9] The exhibit is moving, not only with respect to Martin, but also to other often forgotten buglers and their importance.

During his detailed 1906 interview with a reporter from the *New York Evening Post*, a more personal side of John Martin was revealed. "I was born for a soldier," he told the reporter, "and I love the life. The best times I ever had were on the field, and I often think of the old days with longing." The reporter noted the fire in Martin's eyes when he spoke of his campaigns. The article concluded with the final entry in Martin's diary:

> 'I am now 51 yrs of age on my next birthday ... for the remainder of these few years which I have to spend in this world, I hope I shall be able to spend in peace and happiness with all my friends.' He signed it: 'Most sincerely yours, John D. Martin, Sergt. U.S.A. (retired)'[10]

A soldier's true worth is best judged by his comrades, and not by the critiques and assessments of latter day historians. 'Bugler' Martin was held in high regard by the men he served with, respected for his actions and demeanor. They sometimes affectionately referred to him as 'Dry Martini.'[11] Garnered from the many articles on Martin is the oft-repeated comment on his cheerful and bright attitude. "Martini (sic) was a salty little Italian who had been a drummer boy with Garibaldi in the fight for Italian independence," Private Charles Windolph wrote a few years after the battle, "We used to tease him a lot but we never did after this fight. He proved he was plenty man."[12] The German-born Windolph, wounded during the battle, earned a Medal of Honor for his heroism throughout the two-day engagement. Few could contest the courageous Windolph's opinion of any man.

Colonel Graham interviewed Martin extensively in 1922. He considered Martin "a rather remarkable old soldier, who never misses an occasion to honor the Stars and Stripes, and who turns out in the old blue [uniform], his left arm literally covered to the elbow with service stripes, every time the call of patriotism sounds, whether it be to honor the dead or greet the living." The series of interviews with Graham concluded a few months before Martin's death, and Graham added a fitting epitaph: John Martin, he wrote, "... is well worthy of your respectful attention."[13] Journalist and author Pasquale Petrocelli wisely offered that, in Martin, "... we do not find a hero per se, but rather a normal man. One with qualities both good and bad.

He very much represents the humble and rarely acknowledged aspects of the Italian immigrants of his era, who also worked and sacrificed for their adopted homeland."[14]

From those early uncertain days in Sala until his last breath in a Brooklyn hospital room, Martin's life was perhaps guided by fate. When he needed a name, Mayor Fedele Alliegro provided one. Francesco and Mariantonia Botta gave him a home, while Giuseppe Garibaldi offered adventure. In America, he found hope and in the Army, a new life and name. The Little Bighorn bestowed upon him the celebrity and fame he could never have hoped to achieve as a *trovatello*. John Martin lived an historical odyssey, and his adventures and experiences may likely remain unparalleled. His life spanned both the ancient and modern world, and included a side trip to the Wild West. For most, however, his life is summed up in one imperfect statement: the last white man to see Custer alive.

APPENDIX ONE

The Last Message

Penned by Cooke and carried by Martin, Custer's last order - "Be Quick. Bring pacs." - remains arguably the most famous dispatch in American military history. The last message is on permanent display in the West Point Museum of the United States Military Academy. After he interviewed Martin, Colonel William A. Graham searched for the original dispatch - without success - until 1923 when he met Major Fred Benteen, the son of Captain Frederick Benteen. The Major related, "The famous message with many another relic of the Little Bighorn had then gone up in smoke" during a house fire years earlier. Captain Benteen produced the original message "to supplement his testimony before the Court of Inquiry" in 1879. Afterwards, Graham learned, Benteen gave the original to "a certain Captain Price [possibly George F. Price, a career cavalry officer] of Philadelphia." Graham's dogged efforts revealed that after acquiring the message from Price, a New Jersey collector advertised its sale at an auction.

"Through the commendable efforts of Colonel Charles Francis Bates," Graham wrote of the officer who purchased the original message, "it now rests safe in the library at West Point." Graham asserted the document's authenticity. "Not only is the script of the message itself plainly the hand of Lt. W. W. Cooke," he noted, "... but the unmistakable penmanship of [Captain Frederick] Benteen himself, once seen, never forgotten, attests its genuineness in the 'translation' made for his friend Price's benefit, and which he inscribed above its pencilled [sic] words."[1]

The message's dimensions and condition, as described by the Museum's Curator of Art:

- It measures 8 inches by 4.8 inches.
- The message seems to have been torn from a notebook (or field order pad).
- The words that appear in the center of the page were written in pencil [by Cooke], but the addendum at the top right was penned with sepia ink [by Benteen].

APPENDIX TWO

The *Other* John Martin

While researching John Martin's life after he arrived in America, a different John Martin invariably surfaces. There are several similarities in their tales. John Albert Martin - the *other* John Martin - was born in England in 1849. While crossing the Atlantic a few years later, his parents were lost when the steamer sank and he was placed in a Cleveland orphanage. In 1872, John A. Martin, a resident of the Arizona territory, joined the U.S. Army and assigned to General George Crook's Fifth Cavalry; Martin mustered out in 1877 after completing his five-year enlistment. Army records indicate that he had light-colored hair, a fair complexion, blue eyes, stood 5' 5", and weighed approximately 150 pounds. Physically, he was similar to Giovanni Martino in height and weight, but their differing hair and eye color - and complexion - would have made each distinguishable.

The similarity of their names, and the fact that both served in the U.S. Cavalry during the same period, created conflicting and confused accounts. According to John A. Martin, he became a mail carrier with the Pony Express until 1882. One year later, he moved to Indiana and at the age of 39, he married the much younger Virtue (or Virtu) Cole. Martin died in 1928 and he was buried at Oak Hill Cemetery in Plymouth, Indiana. A plaque placed on his tombstone bears the inscription: *Bearer of Custer's Last Message, Battle of the Little Big Horn.*

Local historians in Plymouth, Cliff and Yvonne Haines, researched John A. Martin's life. They confirmed through a series of censuses that John A. Martin's family resided in Marshall County (Indiana) from 1900 through 1930. The census indicated John A. Martin and Virtue were married in 1889. The 1910 Census listed John A. Martin as a 60-year-old resident of Marshall County (Indiana), and included Virtue as his wife, and their seven children. This John Martin could not have been the same one interviewed in New York City during the same period. The Marshall County Historical Museum in Plymouth noted that the plaque placed on Martin's tombstone many years ago was an error. Kristine Withers, historian and archivist for the U.S. Cavalry Association, opined that John A. Martin's story grew from the simple mistake of their matching surnames. "With the absence of intrusive media coverage of today," she noted, "and with the common knowledge that *a* John Martin carried the last message, his [John A. Martin's] descendants and relatives may have assumed him to be the true last messenger."[1] Unfortunately, John A. Martin may have convinced himself that their tales were true. In June 1926, he claimed to have carried messages to Custer from General Crook's Fifth Cavalry. He added, "... and while I was there, the fight took place." The journalist naively endorsed the false declaration, "Mr. Martin has a nationwide distinction in that he was the last man to speak with General Custer before he went into his fatal battle with the Indians."[2]

Colonel Rodney Thomas of the Little Big Horn Associates established that the Pony Express operated from April 1860 until November 1861; he added that the names of all riders and station operators were recorded, and the only Martin listed is named Robert. Colonel Thomas confirmed that the U.S. Fifth Cavalry was ordered to the Northern Plains *after* the Little Bighorn battle. Assuming John A. Martin was with the Fifth Cavalry in June of 1876, he and his Regiment would have been at least 250 miles away. Throughout the years, surviving Seventh Cavalry officers uniformly agreed that the Italian-born John Martin carried the famous "Be quick" message. Thomas added that Walter Mason Camp confirmed this fact on numerous occasions.[3] Ultimately, however, in light of the many inconsistencies with John Albert Martin's claims as Custer's bugler and last messenger, the late author and researcher Michael Nunnally succinctly closed the argument, "He wasn't."[4]

Notes

Introduction

1 James Donovan, Custer expert and author, in an interview by Johnny D. Boggs, *Wild West section of HistoryNet.com*, April 2, 2009, regarding Donovan's *A Terrible Glory: Custer and the Little Bighorn—the Last Great Battle of the American West*. See Bibliography.

2 Brininstool, *Troopers with Custer : historic incidents of the Battle of the Little Big Horn*, 183.

3 Sklenar, *To Hell With Honor: Custer and the Little Big Horn*, 203.

CHAPTER ONE
A Foundling in Sala

1 A *Comune* is the Italian equivalent of a township or municipality; local government affairs are administered by the Mayor (*Sindaco*), a legislative and executive body.

2 Cole, *Italian Genealogical Records: How to Use Italian Civil, Ecclesiastical & Other Records in Family History Research*, 26.

3 Kertzer, "The lives of foundlings in nineteenth-century Italy," in *Abandoned children*, 41.

4 Ibid., 41.

5 Ibid., 41.

6 Cole, *Italian Genealogical Records*, 26.

7 Kertzer, "The lives of foundlings in nineteenth-century Italy," in *Abandoned children*, 42.

8 Veronesi, *Italian-Americans and Their Communities of Cleveland*, 103.

9 Walsh, "Italian Peasants," in *Our young folk: An Illustrated Magazine for Boys and Girls, Volume 9*, 51-52.

10 Busi correspondence; Colitti correspondence.

11 Cole, *Italian Genealogical Records*, 26.

12 Ibid., 26.

13 Kertzer, "The lives of foundlings in nineteenth-century Italy," in *Abandoned Children*, 50.

14 Cole, *Italian Genealogical Records*, 79.

15 From Pasquale Petrocelli's booklet's, *John Martin: Un Salese a Little Big Horn* (A Sala Man at the Little Big Horn). Petrocelli is a former journalist living in Rome. Before his retirement, he worked for Italy's largest publisher, Arnoldo Mondadori Editore S.p.A. His booklet on Martin's life, privately published with the help of the *Comune* of Sala Consilina in 2005, provided crucial information not previously available. Petrocelli's booklet was provided through the courtesy of Claudio Busi.

16 Veronesi, *Italian-Americans and Their Communities of Cleveland*, 103.

CHAPTER TWO
Searching the Civil Records

1 Giuseppe Colitti is a former professor (docent) of Italian Literature and History living in Sala Consilina (Salerno), Italy. Since his retirement in 1996, Colitti has authored and co-authored several books on the rich oral traditions of southern Italy, primarily for Sala and the Vallo di Diano region. An acknowledged expert in the field, he has participated in many academic conferences including the International Oral History Conference at Columbia University in New York in 1994. Colitti has archived over 2,000 hours of unique audio recordings including songs, proverbs, incantations and prayers. His most recent book, *People and The Risorgimento: Oral Sources of The Vallo di Diano*, was released in 2011. Since 2005, he has served as president of the Center for Study and Research for the Vallo di Diano in Sala Consilina. For more information on Professor Colitti: www.giuseppecolitti.it.

2 Cole, *Italian Genealogical Records*, 16-17.

3 Ibid., 101.

4 Colitti correspondence; Cole, *Italian Genealogical Records*, 145.

5 A former Director of the Comune of Sala Consilina's Office of Business Affairs, Dr. Michele Esposito co-authored *La Sala: Guida storica artistica etnografica"* (Sala: Historical Ethnographic Art Guide). Esposito remains active in cultural affairs for the *comune*, and serves as Secretary at Sala's Center for Study and Research.

6 Petrocelli, Pasquale, *John Martin: Un Salese a Little Big Horn,* Chapter 1.

7 Ibid.

8 Claudio Busi is a freelance researcher and historian living on Bologna, Italy. He has worked with many Universities and private cultural associations on various research projects including Egyptology and prehistoric archeology. He retains membership in the Archaeological Mission in Egypt of the Centre for Egyptology and the Speleological Groups of Bologna. He has maintained an active interest in Italian immigrants in America, spurred by his first visit to America in 1981. Claudio is currently completing the biography of Felice Pedroni (Felix Pedro), the man who first discovered gold in Fairbanks, Alaska. Busi's efforts and contributions to the research on Martino's life are invaluable.

9 Data obtained from the CastleGarden.org site.

10 Kertzer, "The lives of foundlings in nineteenth-century Italy," in *Abandoned Children*, 43.

11 Antonio Castronuovo (41 years old) and Domenico Barrese (61 years old).

12 Kertzer, "The lives of foundlings in nineteenth-century Italy," in *Abandoned Children*, 47.

13 Ibid., 50.

14 Camp, *Custer in '76: Walter Camp's Notes on the Custer Fight*, 99. A respected author, railroad expert and historical researcher, Walter Mason Camp's interest in the Little Bighorn led him to many of the battle's participants, and his extensive interviews of white troopers and American Indian warriors were documented in a collection of detailed notes (currently held in public collections at several Universities and Libraries. He interviewed John Martin in 1908 and 1910.

15 Graham, "The Lost is Found: Custer's Last Message Comes to Light," *Cavalry Journal* 51 (1942), 296-300. Colonel William A. Graham (U.S. Army, retired), an attorney and former member of the Judge Advocate General's office, conducted extensive research on the Little Bighorn, from interviews with the battle's participants to collecting and analyzing original source materials. He authored numerous books and articles on the battle, including "The Custer Myth: A Source Book of Custeriana" and "The Story Of The Little Big Horn." In 1922, Gra-

ham interviewed Martin three times for an article that was published the following year, and after Martin's death: The *Cavalry Journal* 32 (1923) article entitled, "'Come On! Be Quick! Bring Packs!' Custer's Battle Plan, the Story of His Last Message, as Told by the Man who Carried it."

16 "Martini's (Family) Tree Grows in Brooklyn (Md.)," *The Baltimore News-American*, August 1, 1976; Patricia Gordon Ditch correspondence.

17 Graham, "The Lost is Found: Custer's Last Message Comes to Light," *Cavalry Journal* 51 (1942), 298.

CHAPTER THREE
The *Contadini*

1   Gambino, "The Family System," in *The Review of Italian American Studies*, 19.

2   Ibid., 19.

3   The Unification (or, *il Risorgimento*) was the long political movement that merged the disparate states and principalities of the Italian peninsula into a single state in the 1870s.

4   Veronesi, *Italian-Americans and Their Communities of Cleveland*, 102.

5   Ibid., 104.

6   Ibid., 103.

7   Walsh, "Italian Peasants," in *Our young folk: An Illustrated Magazine for Boys and Girls, Volume 9*, 51-52.

8   Cole, *Italian Genealogical Records*, 5.

9   Gambino, "The Family System," in *The Review of Italian American Studies*, 19.

10 Cole, *Italian Genealogical Records*, 4.

11 Gambino, "The Family System," in *The Review of Italian American Studies*, 19.

12 Walsh, "Italian Peasants," in *Our young folk: An Illustrated Magazine for Boys and Girls, Volume 9*, 51-52.

13 Ibid., 51-52.

14 Ibid., 51-52: "The reason this oven is made so large is, that bread is baked in it only about once every three months, and, therefore, enough has to be baked at one time to until the next bake-day comes round."

15 Ibid., 52.

16 Professor Colitti noted that, "... at the time of Martin and until the 1950s, there were few houses with running water" in the Campania region. In light of the ages of the homes and their placement within many hilltop towns, the addition of plumbing proved quite difficult to install retroactively.

17 Walsh, "Italian Peasants," in *Our young folk: An Illustrated Magazine for Boys and Girls, Volume 9*, 52.

18 Gambino, "The Family System," in *The Review of Italian American Studies*, 19.

19 Walsh, "Italian Peasants," in *Our young folk: An Illustrated Magazine for Boys and Girls, Volume 9*, 52.

20 Ibid., 52.

21 Kertzer, "The lives of foundlings in nineteenth-century Italy," in *Abandoned Children*, 46.

22 Walsh, "Italian Peasants," in *Our young folk: An Illustrated Magazine for Boys and Girls, Volume 9*, 52.

23 Veronesi, *Italian-Americans and Their Communities of Cleveland*, 143-144.

24 Scarpaci and Mormino, *The Journey of the Italians in America*, 16.

CHAPTER FOUR
From Garibaldi to America

1 Petrocelli, *John Martin: Un Salese a Little Big Horn*, Chapter 1.

2 Ibid.

3 Forbes, *The Campaign of Garibaldi in the Two Sicilies: A Personal Narrative*, 227.

4 "Custer's bugler: 'Ticket Chopper'," *The Evening Post (New York)*, September 15, 1906.

5 Graham, "'Come On! Be Quick! Bring Packs!' Custer's Battle Plan, the Story of His Last Message, as Told by the Man who Carried it," *Cavalry Journal* 32 (1923), 287.

6 Petrocelli, *John Martin: Un Salese a Little Big Horn*, Chapter 1.

7 From journalist Romulus Amicarella's *Fighting for the Italian independence of the province of Salerno*. Information provided by Giuseppe Colitti via personal correspondence.

8 Scarpaci and Mormino, *The Journey of the Italians in America*, 27.

9 Petrocelli, *John Martin: Un Salese a Little Big Horn*, Chapter 2.

10 Ibid.
11 "Custer's bugler: 'Ticket Chopper'," *The Evening Post (New York)*, September 15, 1906.
12 Petrocelli, *John Martin: Un Salese a Little Big Horn*, Chapter 2.
13 Scarpaci and Mormino, *The Journey of the Italians in America*, 27-28.
14 Moreno, "Castle Garden: The Forgotten Gateway," *Ancestry Magazine* 21, no. 2 (2003), 42.
15 Ibid., 42.
16 Ibid., 43.

CHAPTER FIVE
Bugler Martin

1 Rhodes, *History of the United States*, 41.
2 Ibid., 43.
3 Donovan, *A Terrible Glory*, 122.
4 Veronesi, *Italian-Americans and Their Communities of Cleveland*, 113.
5 From Veronesi, *Italian-Americans and Their Communities of Cleveland*, 121: "In general, northern Europeans - mostly Protestant and often from Germany and various Scandinavian countries - met less resistance than their darker-skinned counterparts from southern Europe."
6 Petrocelli, *John Martin: Un Salese a Little Big Horn*, Chapter 2.
7 Ibid.
8 Donovan, *A Terrible Glory*, 122.
9 Petrocelli, *John Martin: Un Salese a Little Big Horn*, Chapter 2.
10 Donovan, *A Terrible Glory*, 122.
11 De Voto, Martin and De Rudio survived the Battle of the Little Bighorn. The remaining three Italians were not present for the battle: Vinatieri remained at a base camp with the regimental band; James was detailed on temporary assignment to another unit; and, Lombard recuperated in the hospital at Fort Abraham Lincoln from an unspecified illness or injury.
12 Katcher and Volstad, *US cavalry on the plains 1850-90*, 23.
13 Ibid.
14 Ibid., 22.
15 Donovan, *A Tragic Glory*, 121.

16 Katcher and Volstad, *US cavalry on the plains 1850-90*, 22.
17 Donovan, *A Tragic Glory*, 121.
18 Robinson III, *A Good Year to Die*, 188.
19 Katcher and Volstad, *US cavalry on the plains 1850-90*, 24.
20 Ibid.
21 Sklenar, *To Hell With Honor: Custer and the Little Big Horn*, 65.

CHAPTER SIX
Custer and the Indians

1 Brininstool, *Troopers with Custer : Historic incidents of the Battle of the Little Big Horn*, 186.
2 Donovan, *A Terrible Glory*, 55.

CHAPTER SEVEN
The Campaign

1 "Custer's bugler: 'Ticket Chopper'," *The Evening Post (New York)*, September 15, 1906.
2 Accompanying the command were a number of Arikara, Osage, and Crow Indian scouts. Some tribes like the Arikara and Crow decided that allying with the Army would provide better opportunities in reclaiming land and ponies taken by the aggressive Lakota.
3 Goodrich, *Scalp dance: Indian warfare on the high plains*, 222.
4 "Custer's bugler: 'Ticket Chopper'," *The Evening Post (New York)*, September 15, 1906.
5 Ibid.
6 Godfrey, "Custer's Last Battle," *The Century Illustrated Monthly Magazine* 18, no. 3 (1892), 367.
7 "Custer's bugler: 'Ticket Chopper'," *The Evening Post (New York)*, September 15, 1906.
8 Godfrey, "Custer's Last Battle," *The Century Illustrated Monthly Magazine* 18, no. 3 (1892), 361.
9 "Custer's bugler: 'Ticket Chopper'," *The Evening Post (New York)*, September 15, 1906.

10   Windolph, The Story of Sergeant Windolph, 85; referencing
     William A. Graham's article, "'Come On! Be Quick! Bring
     Packs!' Custer's Battle Plan, the Story of His Last Message, as
     Told by the Man who Carried it," Cavalry Journal 32 (1923).

11   Godfrey, "Custer's Last Battle," *The Century Illustrated Monthly
     Magazine* 18, no. 3 (1892), 365.

12   Sklenar, *To Hell With Honor: Custer and the Little Big Horn*, 107.

CHAPTER EIGHT
Cooke's Message

1   Windolph, The Story of Sergeant Windolph, 86; referencing
     William A. Graham's article, "'Come On! Be Quick! Bring
     Packs!' Custer's Battle Plan, the Story of His Last Message, as
     Told by the Man who Carried it." *Cavalry Journal* 32 (1923).

2   Ibid., 84; referencing William A. Graham's article, "Come On!
     Be Quick! Bring Packs!" *Cavalry Journal* 32 (1923).

3   Ibid.

4   Ibid.

5   Brininstool, *Troopers with Custer : historic incidents of the Battle of the
     Little Big Horn*, 25.

6   Windolph, The Story of Sergeant Windolph, 85; referencing
     Graham's article, "'Come On! Be Quick! Bring Packs!'" *Cavalry
     Journal* 32 (1923).

7   Donovan, *A Terrible Glory*, 211.

8   "Custer's bugler: 'Ticket Chopper'," *The Evening Post (New
     York)*, September 15, 1906.

9   Windolph, The Story of Sergeant Windolph, 86; referencing
     Graham's article, "'Come On! Be Quick! Bring Packs!'" *Cavalry
     Journal* 32 (1923).

10   Camp, *Custer in '76: Walter Camp's Notes on the Custer Fight*, 101.

11   Windolph, The Story of Sergeant Windolph, 86; referencing
     Graham's article, "'Come On! Be Quick! Bring Packs!'" *Cavalry
     Journal* 32 (1923).

12   "Custer's bugler: 'Ticket Chopper'," *The Evening Post (New
     York)*, September 15, 1906.

13   Windolph, *The Story of Sergeant Windolph*, 87; referencing Gra-
     ham's article, "'Come On! Be Quick! Bring Packs!'" *Cavalry
     Journal* 32 (1923).

14 Ibid.
15 "Custer's bugler: 'Ticket Chopper'," *The Evening Post (New York)*, September 15, 1906.
16 Camp, *Custer in '76: Walter Camp's Notes on the Custer Fight*, 103.
17 The three accounts were told to Colonel William A. Graham in 1922 (over the course of three interviews), Walter Mason Camp (1908 interview), and as noted in his diary, as noted in the article entitled, "Custer's bugler: 'Ticket Chopper'," published in *The Evening Post (New York)* on September 15, 1906.

CHAPTER NINE
Riding to Benteen

1 Windolph, *The Story of Sergeant Windolph*, 88; referencing William A. Graham's article, "'Come On! Be Quick! Bring Packs!' Custer's Battle Plan, the Story of His Last Message, as Told by the Man who Carried it," Cavalry Journal 32 (1923).
2 Ibid.
3 The list included the three Custer brothers - Lieutenant Colonel George Armstrong Custer, Captain Thomas Custer, and Boston Custer - their cousin Henry "Autie" Reed, and a brother-in-law, First Lieutenant James Calhoun.
4 Windolph, *The Story of Sergeant Windolph*, 89; referencing Graham's article, "'Come On! Be Quick! Bring Packs!'" *Cavalry Journal* 32 (1923).
5 Ibid., 88.
6 Camp, *Custer in '76*, 101.
7 Ibid.
8 Windolph, *The Story of Sergeant Windolph*, 88; referencing Graham's article, "'Come On! Be Quick! Bring Packs!'" *Cavalry Journal* 32 (1923).
9 Camp, *Custer in '76*, 101.
10 Sklenar, *To Hell With Honor: Custer and the Little Big Horn*, 232.
11 Graham, "The Lost is Found: Custer's Last Message Comes to Light," *Cavalry Journal* 51 (1942), 296; referencing Benteen's letter to his wife, dated July 4, 1876.
12 Ibid., 297.
13 Sklenar, *To Hell With Honor*, 235.

14 Godfrey, "Custer's Last Battle," *The Century Illustrated Monthly Magazine* 18, no. 3 (1892), 372.

CHAPTER TEN
The Hilltop

1   See Appendix 1: The Last Message.
2   Graham, "The Lost is Found: Custer's Last Message Comes to Light," *Cavalry Journal* 51 (1942), 296; referencing Benteen's letter to his wife, dated July 4, 1876.
3   Camp, *Custer in '76*, 101, 104.
4   Windolph, *The Story of Sergeant Windolph*, 83; referencing Graham's article, "'Come On! Be Quick! Bring Packs!'" *Cavalry Journal* 32 (1923).
5   Graham, "The Lost is Found: Custer's Last Message Comes to Light," *Cavalry Journal* 51 (1942), 298; referencing Benteen's letter to his wife, dated July 4, 1876.
6   Donovan, *A Terrible Glory*, 286.
7   Godfrey, "Custer's Last Battle," *The Century Illustrated Monthly Magazine* 18, no. 3 (1892), 377.
8   Donovan, *A Terrible Glory*, 286.
9   Ibid., 288.
10 Godfrey, "Custer's Last Battle," *The Century Illustrated Monthly Magazine* 18, no. 3 (1892), 377.
11 Ibid., 378.
12 Camp, *Custer in '76*, 101.
13 Ibid., 104.
14 Godfrey, "Custer's Last Battle," *The Century Illustrated Monthly Magazine* 18, no. 3 (1892), 378.
15 Donovan, *A Terrible Glory*, 297.
16 Godfrey, "Custer's Last Battle," *The Century Illustrated Monthly Magazine* 18, no. 3 (1892), 379.
17 From Martin's testimony at the U.S. Army Court of Inquiry's investigation into the Battle of The Little Bighorn. This response by Martin was recorded on January 31, 1879: University of Wisconsin Digital History Collection (Reno Court of Inquiry transcripts, 346, http://digital.library.wisc.edu/1711.dl/ History.Reno.html)

CHAPTER ELEVEN
The Fate of Custer

1   "Custer's bugler: 'Ticket Chopper'," *The Evening Post (New York)*, September 15, 1906.
2   Godfrey, "Custer's Last Battle," *The Century Illustrated Monthly Magazine* 18, no. 3 (1892), 383.
3   Camp, *Custer in '76*, 102.
4   "Custer's bugler: 'Ticket Chopper'," *The Evening Post (New York)*, September 15, 1906.
5   "Too True: The Appalling Tale of Indian Butchery Confirmed," *Chicago Daily Tribune*, July 7, 1876.

CHAPTER TWELVE
The Court of Inquiry

1   A full transcript of Martin's testimony at the U.S. Army Court of Inquiry's investigation into the Battle of The Little Bighorn can be found at the University of Wisconsin Digital History Collection.:
    http://digital.library.wisc.edu/1711.dl/History.Reno.html.
2   Sklenar, *To Hell With Honor: Custer and the Little Big Horn*, 213.
3   Windolph, *The Story of Sergeant Windolph*, 89; referencing Graham's article, "'Come On! Be Quick! Bring Packs!'" *Cavalry Journal* 32 (1923).
4   Sklenar, *To Hell With Honor: Custer and the Little Big Horn*, 213.
5   Camp, *Custer in '76*, 102.
6   James Donovan, interview by Johnny D. Boggs, *Wild West section of HistoryNet.com*, April 2, 2009:
    http://www.historynet.com/interview-with-george-custer-expert-james-donovan.htm/3.
7   Donovan, *A Terrible Glory*, 372.
8   Donovan, interview by Johnny D. Boggs, *Wild West section of HistoryNet.com*, April 2, 2009.
9   "Custer's bugler: 'Ticket Chopper'," *The Evening Post (New York)*, September 15, 1906.

CHAPTER THIRTEEN
Fort McHenry

1   "Custer's bugler: 'Ticket Chopper'," *The Evening Post (New York)*, September 15, 1906.

2   "Sole Survivor of the Custer Massacre," *The Baltimore Sun*, July 4, 1885.

3   "One Of Custer's Soldiers," *New York Times*, October 21, 1886.

4   *Indian Chieftain (Vinita, Indian Territory, Oklahoma)*, March 9, 1893.

5   "Custer's bugler: 'Ticket Chopper'," *The Evening Post (New York)*, September 15, 1906.

6   Ibid.

7   From the United States Census records for military and naval personnel (dated June 1, 1900).

8   "Custer's bugler: 'Ticket Chopper'," *The Evening Post (New York)*, September 15, 1906.

CHAPTER FOURTEEN
Trading Baltimore for Brooklyn

1   A few newspaper accounts referred to their store as a refreshment stand.

2   "Custer's bugler: 'Ticket Chopper'," *The Evening Post (New York)*, September 15, 1906.

3   Kennedy, "Tunnel Vision: He Was Custer's Bugler. Then, the Subway Called," *New York Times*, July 29, 2003.

4   The *Brooklyn Standard Union's* editor appended a brief note to a 1906 article that listed Martin's local address as 58 York Street; a fellow Seventh Regiment veteran, Henry Petring, a Private with Company G, asked the newspaper for help in locating Martin. Both Petring and Martin fought and survived the hilltop siege at the Little Bighorn.

5   "Custer's bugler: 'Ticket Chopper'," *The Evening Post (New York)*, September 15, 1906.

6   "'Bugler' Martin, In Company With A Number Of Other Veterans," *Brooklyn Standard Union*, June 24, 1906.

7 "'Bugler' Martin, In Company With A Number Of Other Veterans, Will Play 'Taps' Over The Grave Of The Famous Indian Fighter," *Brooklyn Standard Union*, June 24, 1906.

8 Ibid.

9 *National Tribune (Washington, D.C.)*, August 6, 1906.

10 "Sole Survivor of The Custer Massacre," *Minneapolis Journal*, July 29, 1906.

11 "Custer's bugler: 'Ticket Chopper'," *The Evening Post (New York)*, September 15, 1906.

12 "Custer's bugler: 'Ticket Chopper'," *The Evening Post (New York)*, September 15, 1906.

13 "Sole Survivor of The Custer Massacre," *Minneapolis Journal*, July 29, 1906.

14 "'Bugler' Martin, In Company With A Number Of Other Veterans," *Brooklyn Standard Union*, June 24, 1906.

15 "Will Arrest Speculators," in *Amusement Notes, New York Times*, February 6, 1907.

16 "Philadelphia Opera Plan," in *Amusement Notes, New York Times*, April 30, 1907.

17 Ibid.

18 "Custer Reunion at Canandaigua," *Geneva Daily Times (New York)*, August 20, 1907.

19 "Tunnel Vision: He Was Custer's Bugler. Then, the Subway Called," *New York Times*, July 29, 2003; referencing *The Brooklyn Eagle* article entitled, "Man Who Narrowly Escapes Lava Beds Massacre – Wanted by Deserted Wife," 1908.

20 Petrocelli, *John Martin: Un Salese a Little Big Horn*, Chapter 5.

21 Caniglia, "John Martin Makes The New York Times." *The Little Bighorn History Associates Newsletter* 38, no. 2 (2004): 4; referencing *The Brooklyn Eagle* article entitled, "Man Who Narrowly Escapes Lava Beds Massacre – Wanted by Deserted Wife," 1908.

22 The title of the article itself is erroneous (re: "Man Who Narrowly Escapes Lava Beds Massacre"); Martino had not enlisted in the Army when the Modoc War (or "Lava Beds War") took place in 1872-1873. Nevertheless a sufficient amount of verifiable facts was included, perhaps an indication of sloppy rather than misleading journalism.

23 Ibid., 4-5; The granddaughters interviewed in Baltimore, Maryland by Salvatore Caniglia in 1978 were Bessie Hartman (the

daughter of Julia Martin) and Margaret Allison, Mae's daughter. Both were living in Baltimore at the time of their interview. Following in Aunt Bessie's footsteps to keep the Martin story alive is her niece, and John Martin's great-granddaughter, Patricia Gordon Ditch. Her father, Joseph Gordon, was Julia Martin's son. "There were many Sundays spent at my Aunt Bessie's house," Patricia Ditch recalled, "and I heard my father's uncles' stories about pap [John Martin]." Patricia Ditch has served as a conduit for this author, helping to connect disparate researchers from two continents including Claudio Busi, and her assistance throughout the project is greatly appreciated.

24 Although Baltimore boasted a sizeable Italian population, many more Italians made Brooklyn their home; the New York borough may have been a favorite destination for immigrants from Sala, and perhaps he missed hearing the Campania dialect of his youth.

25 "Custer survivor Tells of Massacre," *The Brooklyn Daily Eagle*, April 4, 1914.

26 "Custer Survivor In Line," *New York Tribune*, April 27, 1918.

27 *The Brooklyn Daily Eagle*, May 13, 1918.

28 1920 U.S. Census records found on FamilySearch.org.

29 Caniglia, "John Martin Makes The New York Times." *The Little Bighorn History Associates Newsletter* 38, no. 2 (2004): 4; referencing *The Brooklyn Eagle* article entitled, "Man Who Narrowly Escapes Lava Beds Massacre – Wanted by Deserted Wife," 1908.

CHAPTER FIFTEEN
Taps

1 "John Martin, Last Survivor of Custer Massacre, is Dead," *The Brooklyn Daily Eagle*, December 26, 1922.

2 Grave 8865, Section 2.

3 Ron Hartman's grandmother, Julia, was the oldest daughter of John and Julia Martin.

4 Personal correspondence with W. Donald Horn.

5 Sklenar, *To Hell With Honor: Custer and the Little Big Horn*, 213.

6 Ibid., 203.

7   Ibid., 197.
8   Graham, "The Lost is Found: Custer's Last Message Comes to Light," *Cavalry Journal* 51 (1942), 299.
9   Jari Villanueva is the foremost authority on the bugle call 'Taps' and has studied the use of the bugle in the United States military for over twenty years. Prior to his retirement, Jari was a member of the United States Air Force Band where he spent 23 years sounding 'Taps' at the Arlington National Cemetery. He continues to study music as a Brass and bugle Historian and maintains the Taps Project at the Arlington National Cemetery (Tapsbugler.com).
10   "Custer's bugler: 'Ticket Chopper'," *The Evening Post (New York)*, September 15, 1906.
11   Donovan, *A Terrible Glory*, 211.
12   Windolph, *The Story of Sergeant Windolph*, 83.
13   Graham, "The Lost is Found: Custer's Last Message Comes to Light," *Cavalry Journal* 51 (1942), 300.
14   Petrocelli, *John Martin: Un Salese a Little Big Horn*, Epilogue.

APPENDIX ONE
The Last Message

1   Graham, William A. "The Lost is Found: Custer's Last Message Comes to Light," *Cavalry Journal* 51 (1942): 296-300.

APPENDIX TWO
The *Other* John Martin

1   Personal correspondence with Kristine Withers.
2   *The Plymouth Daily Democrat (Indiana)*, June 5, 1926.
3   Personal correspondence with Colonel Rodney G. Thomas, U.S. Army (retired).
4   Nunnally, "Custer Survivors in Little Bighorn Folklore." *Little Bighorn History Alliance*. April 26, 2010. (http://Littlebighorn.wetpaint.com/page/Survivors+in+Bigh orn+Folklore)

Bibliography

Books

Brininstool. E.A. *Troopers with Custer : historic incidents of the Battle of the Little Big Horn.* Mechanicsburg, PA: Stackpole Books, 1994.

Camp, Walter Mason. *Custer in '76: Walter Camp's Notes on the Custer Fight,* edited by Kenneth M. Hammer. Provo, Utah: Brigham Young University Press, 1976.

Cole, Trafford R. *Italian Genealogical Records: How to Use Italian Civil, Ecclesiastical & Other Records in Family History Research.* Salt Lake City: Ancestry Publishing, 1995.

Donovan, James. *A Terrible Glory: Custer and the Little Bighorn—the Last Great Battle of the American West.* New York: Little, Brown and Company, 2008.

Forbes, Charles Stuart. *The Campaign of Garibaldi in the Two Sicilies: A Personal Narrative.* Edinburgh: W. Blackwood and sons, 1861.

Goodrich. Thomas. *Scalp dance: Indian warfare on the high plains, 1865-1879.* Mechanicsburg, PA: Stackpole Books, 2002.

Graham, William A. and Fred Dustin. *The Custer Myth: a Source Book of Custeriana.* Harrisburg, PA: Stackpole Co., 1953.

Katcher, Philip R. N. and Ron Volstad. *US cavalry on the plains 1850-90.* London, UK: Osprey, 1985.

Kertzer, David I. "The lives of foundlings in nineteenth-century Italy." In *Abandoned Children,* edited by Catherine Panter-Brick and Malcolm T. Smith. Cambridge, UK; New York, NY, USA: Cambridge University Press, 2000.

Petrocelli, Pasquale, *John Martin: Un Salese a Little Big Horn* (A Sala Man at the Little Big Horn) Italy: Self-published booklet, 2005.

Rhodes, James Ford. *History of the United States: From The Compromise of 1850 To The Final Restoration of Home Rule at the South in 1877 - Volume 7 (1872-1877).* New York: The MacMillan Company, 1906.

Robinson III, Charles M. *A Good Year to Die: The Story of the Great Sioux War.* New York: Random House, 1995.

Scarpaci, Vincenza and Gary R. Mormino. *The Journey of the Italians in America.* Gretna, LA: Pelican Publishing Co., 2008.

Sklenar, Larry. *To Hell With Honor: Custer and the Little Big Horn.* Norman: University of Oklahoma Press, 2000.

Sorrentino, Frank M. and Jerome Krase. *The Review of Italian American Studies*. Edited by Frank M. Sorrentino and Jerome Krase. Lanham, MD: Lexington Books, 2000.

Veronesi, Gene P. *Italian-Americans and Their Communities of Cleveland.* Cleveland, OH: Cleveland State University, 1977.

Walsh, Wm. S. *Our young folk: An Illustrated Magazine for Boys and Girls, Volume 9.* Edited by John Townsend Trowbridge and Lucy Larcom. Boston: James R. Osgood & Company, 1873.

Windolph, Charles. *The Story of Sergeant Windolph, Last Survivor of the Battle of the Little Big Horn.* As told to Frazier and Robert Hunt. Lincoln: University of Nebraska Press, 1987.

Articles

Caniglia, Salvatore A. "John Martin Makes The New York Times." *The Little Bighorn History Associates Newsletter* 38, no. 2 (2004).

Godfrey, Edward S. "Custer's Last Battle," *The Century Illustrated Monthly Magazine* 18, no. 3 (1892).

Graham, William A. "'Come On! Be Quick! Bring Packs!' Custer's Battle Plan, the Story of His Last Message, as Told by the Man who Carried it," *Cavalry Journal* 32 (1923).

———. "The Lost is Found: Custer's Last Message Comes to Light," *Cavalry Journal* 51 (1942).

Moreno, Barry. "Castle Garden: The Forgotten Gateway," *Ancestry Magazine* 21, no. 2 (2003).

Nunnally, Michael L. "Custer Survivors in Little Bighorn Folklore." *Little Bighorn History Alliance.* April 26, 2010, http://littlebighorn .wetpaint.com/page/Survivors+in+Bighorn+Folklore.html.

Newspapers

Baltimore News-American
Baltimore Sun
Brooklyn (Daily) Eagle
Brooklyn Standard Union
Chicago Daily Tribune
Evening Post (New York)
Geneva Daily Times (New York)
Indian Chieftain (Indian Territory, Oklahoma)
Minneapolis Journal
National Tribune (Washington, D.C.)
New York Times
New York Tribune

Omaha Daily Bee
Plymouth Daily Democrat (Indiana)

Other Sources
Donovan, James. "Interview with George Custer Expert James Donovan," *Wild West section of HistoryNet.com*. By Johnny D. Boggs, http://www.historynet.com/interview-with-george-custer-expert-james-donovan.html.
Reno Court of Inquiry transcripts: University of Wisconsin Digital History Collection, http://digital.library.wisc.edu/17 1 1.dl/History.Reno
The Battery Conservancy (re: CastleGarden.org database of immigration records), http://www.castlegarden.org.

Personal Correspondence
Busi, Claudio
Colitti, Giuseppe
Ditch, Patricia Gordon
Donahue, Michael
Esposito, Michele
Haines, Cliff and Yvonne
Horn, W. Donald
Thomas, Rodney H.
Villanueva, Jari
Withers, Kristine

CPSIA information can be obtained at www.ICGtesting.com
Printed in the USA
LVOW01s1116261013

358715LV00003B/150/P